The Retired Millennial

A Simple Path to Financial Freedom for Generation Y

Alex Howell

Copyright ©2016 by Alex Howell

ISBN number if you have it.

Alex Howell (or company name)
Address line one.
Address line 2
City Missouri zip

Phone if desired
email

alexanderhowell.com

Cover photo credit, other photos credit (most will go in copy with picture if included).

Special Thank you to ?

You can add an about the author info here as well or at the end where I currently added a section.

Table of Contents

What if you didn't have to keep working that old nine to five drag?

What if your life could change for good?

What if you had the money you needed right now?

What if...

Here's the thing, in today's world, we all know that it takes work, and a lot of it, to make money. As a result, many people work their fingers to the bone until they are 65-70 years old before they can consider retirement. Some are never even able to retire.

And, no matter the case, when does living start? How can you possibly do all the things you want when you are 70? That's no way to live life. It just doesn't make sense that this would be the standard.

That's where a better option comes in.

Become a retired Millennial.

What???

I know that is what you are thinking right now.

How can I retire at my age?

Well, that's exactly what we are going to talk about in this book.

Defining the Generations

But first, who or what is a Millennial? And what do we mean by "generations"?

Referring to generations is a shorthand method for referencing when someone was born and lumping all persons from that generation into certain characteristics. Truth-be-told, problems often arise when trying to label anything, but they still offer useful guidance for classification and comparison between the generations – also known as generational gaps.

Millennial is the nickname assigned to a person that grew up with the technology that we're still employing today. This can generally include those born somewhere in a range from the early 1980s to 2000s. Great debate has existed as to which birth years constitute this generation, as well as other. Millennials are also referred to as Generation Y.

Interestingly, a search on the Internet just five years ago listed Generation Y and Millennial as separate shorter generations with different characteristics. Now, however, William Schroer, The Social Librarian, as well as others, lists them as one clear generation with merged classifications. For purposes herein, his dates and characteristic details will work as a baseline in the chart below.

Generation Name	Birth Range	Key Traits
Depression Era	1912-1921	conservative, savers, low debt, legacy-driven, patriotic, work-oriented, respect for authority, moral obligation
World War II	1922-1927	collectively oriented with a "deferment" ideology rather and "me", hard workers
Post-War Cohort	1928-1945	experienced great job opportunities, discomfort and uncertainty, security-driven, preference for the familiar
Boomers I The Baby Boomers	1946-1954	good economic opportunities, largely optimistic, either served in or protested the Vietnam War
Boomers II Generation Jones	1955-1965	faced societal economic struggles, sense of "I'm out for me", narcissistic, self-help oriented, skeptical of media, lived in shadow of Boomers I
Generation X	1966-1976	the "lost" generation, "latchkey" kids, life muddled with divorce and daycare, skeptics, "what's in it for me", best educated generation, family planning is high, wait for family-building, great concern to avoid broken homes
Generation Y Echo Boomers Millenniums	1977-1994	largest generation since Baby Boomers, sophisticated, technology-wise, exposure to intense media makes them insusceptible to traditional marketing, ethnically diverse, segmented due to rise in social media, brand loyal, flexible, changes fashion often, style conscious, involved in financial decisions early
Generation Z	1995-2012?	a lot of unknowns, diverse environment, high levels of technology, accelerated achievement opportunities available, refocus on education, customized instruction, highly sophisticated with media, computer oriented, Internet savvy, still evolving

While the main audience for this book is the Millennial generation – there is a lot that can be of benefit to everyone from any generation. Not only that, but understanding where each generation is coming from helps to shape the understanding of the next generation.

Okay, to really explain a retired Millennial, let's break those two words down.

According to the dictionary, Retired means "withdrawn from or no longer occupied with one's business or profession."

To further understand the Millennial, Philip Bump tells us that "in October, 2004, researchers Neil Howe and William Strauss called Millennials the 'next great generation,' which is funny. They define the group 'as those born in 1982 and approximately 20 years thereafter.' In 2012, they affixed the end point as 2004." Do note that the dates here are different from those in the chart above, which only speaks further to the debate over the when and who for each generation.

Now, allow me to get totally sidetracked here for a second. It says it is funny that a Millennial would be called the next great generation. Why? Well, some people don't think so highly of us and we have gotten a reputation we actually don't deserve. We are the next great generation and we have amazing potential.

And, that is what I want to tap into in this book: our potential – How we can use our potential to become "retired" long before the traditional age.

The Purpose

So then, what's the purpose of this book, exactly?

We can become financially free in order to obtain freedom of choice in our lives.

Right now, you can't choose things. You don't get to make decisions – your job does. Your job dictates everything you do from what you eat to the type of house you live in to when and where you can take vacations. It really isn't fair that you are tied down like that.

And, that's how we get to the purpose of this book – you can become 100% totally financially free. And, when you do, you get to make all the decisions:

- You can live in the type of house you want to.

- You can choose to live in the city you would like (or the countryside if you prefer).

- You can choose when you go on vacation, where you go, and how long you stay.

- You can choose how to live your life, completely for you and your family.

As a Retired Millennial, you get to make all of the decisions.

I will take you step-by-step through the process. Let's begin.

Zero Debt

It really is that simple.

You have to find your way to zero debt. When you don't owe anything, guess what can happen? Every single cent you make is profit.

You don't waste your time paying bills anymore.

You don't owe money.

Sounds pretty damn fantastic doesn't it?

Becoming the Retired Millennial is all about getting to zero debt. And, that's a big part of what we are going to talk about.

Financial Freedom

So, what do you think comes from zero debt?

If you answered financial freedom, then I like the way you think.

That's because it's how I think too. When you aren't bound to debts, then you take charge of your life and everything changes.

We are going to talk about how to make financial freedom actually happen:

- How to develop passive income that is greater or equal to all expenses in a given month.

- How to develop passive income that is truly passive (as in you don't have to do a thing – the money just gets deposited).

- How to develop work from anywhere – income earned from working on something you are truly passionate about and allowing you to do whatever you want.

- How to enjoy a goal of being able to work for fun and not having to worry about income.

That's what financial freedom is all about. And that is when life truly begins – when you can do what you love and work for fun.

Concentrates on Cash Flow

When it comes to getting to where you can retire now rather than later, everything that matters comes from cash flow. Cash flow is king and that is something I just cannot stress enough.

We are going to talk a lot about different ways you can invest your money and how you need to make sure your investments are appreciating – that's how you have a sound investment that will ensure you reach what we like to call "The New Retirement".

Your goal, and mine for that matter, is to create streams of income that replace your working income.

Why?

Well, it's simple. When you do, you never have to "work" again.

The Difference in Active and Passive Income

It's vital that you understand the difference between active and passive income because our goal here is to earn *passive income*. Once you reach that point – that's when you get the life that you have always wanted.

Active Income

Active income is what you are likely doing right now. When you go to a job, deal with the "old grind" and get home exhausted, then you are dealing with active income. Here are its traits:

- YOU have to WORK for the money.

- You work and you get paid a salary.

- It's work for pay.

- If you have a job, then you are making active income.

"Well, isn't that how we all make money?" you ask.

If you look at the world like you have been told to look at it, then yes. If you look at the world differently – in the way I want you to see it, then no. My way involves passive income.

Passive Income

Passive income is different. It doesn't come from the traditional means and it doesn't require that you go into the same old job day in and day out. Here are its characteristics:

- It is MONEY that works FOR you.

- It is income you get from assets that you have purchased either with your active income or other passive income you have accrued.

- You can create businesses that will earn passive income for you.

Passive income is sort of the opposite of what you think you have to do to make money. Once you go through this book and take action, you are going to learn how to pay off debt and then just live your life doing things you love while enjoying passive income to one degree or another.

But, it is going to take you looking at things in a different way from what you have been told over and over again throughout life. All of your life, you have been told that you have to work to survive:

Work your fingers to the bone.

Go to the old grindstone again.

Break your back making money.

These are the types of phrases you have heard again and again. That's because this is what you think you are supposed to do and it's what society tells you that you are supposed to do.

Changing your perspective may be a little difficult in the beginning. After all, these thoughts have been ingrained in your mind from all of the generations before you. But, when you do change your perspective and you recognize that there is another way, then you will free yourself from those old ways.

It's about time, don't you think?

Getting to Financial Freedom

We are going to get to this a lot more later, but for now, I want to put it to you in the most simplistic terms. How do you get to financial freedom? It takes just a few steps on a basic path:

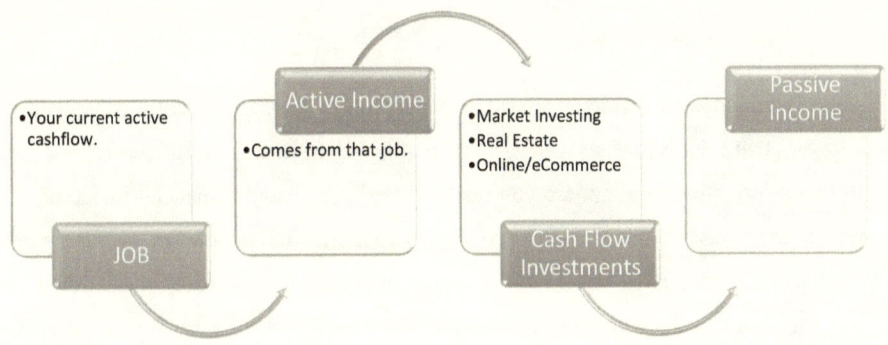

That's your path to financial freedom. It is actually a simple path when you break it down this way. But, like I mentioned, there is much more to it and we are going to talk about everything throughout this book.

So, if you are ready to delve in and find out how you can change your life for good, then let's get started.

But, before we get into all the good stuff, we will talk about the problems you may think that you face as a Millennial. That's because I want to get something clear right away:

None of those problems have to be an issue.

None of them are actually problems that will slow you down.

Let's get started, though, and get those issues out of the way...

Chapter One:

Issues Facing Millennials When First Entering the Job Market

We have defined who we are – an entire generation of people, currently described by a few stereotypes that I don't love, as well as a few that make us stand out from generations past. Now, with that information in mind, are you ready to find your way to financial freedom? In reality, you have to understand the problems standing in your way before you can clear them out, right? Well, that means we have to talk about some things that will probably make you feel a little down. But, don't let them get to you. I promise they are all problems that we can overcome.

High Unemployment Rate (Especially for Millennials)

In the past couple of years, the unemployment rate has actually gone down. In fact, according to the United States Department of Labor's Bureau of Labor Statistics, the unemployment rate for the United States in June of 2015 was 5.3%. That is down over the last few years, but the job market hit a spike that has caused repercussions that the Millennial Generation is still experiencing today.

Here's some numbers to give you a better idea of what I'm talking about. Below are the unemployment rates for the month of June for the past few years:

- 2009 – 9.5%
- 2010 – 9.4%
- 2011 – 9.1%
- 2012 – 8.2%
- 2013 – 7.5%
- 2014 – 6.1%

While the rate has been going down, that doesn't mean that jobs are readily available. Want to overcome that problem? Make yourself look amazing. What do I mean by that? Stay tuned to find out!

The "unemployment problem" hit Generation Y especially hard. That's because when companies aren't hiring, they tend to keep their experienced employees instead of bringing on new ones. Fact is, new employees cost more money to train and prepare for position and while we like to think that a Millennial brings efficiency to the forefront – tradition normally wins over being outside-the-box. However, we're nothing if not savvy, so it's all about standing out beyond that bottom line.

Speaking of experienced employees…

Baby Boomers Are STILL Working

There just aren't as many positions available. After all, while the population is still growing, people are choosing to stay at their jobs for much longer. The Baby Boomers (the generation of people collectively born between 1946 and 1965 – and there are a lot of them, hence their nickname) are choosing to wait longer and longer before they retire because they know they need more money in order to live comfortably in their golden years.

> *"The first wave of the generation became eligible for early retirement under Social Security about six years ago, yet Boomers still comprise roughly one third of the workforce.*
>
> *Nearly half of all Baby Boomers still working today say they don't expect to retire until they are 66 or older, according to a Gallup poll. One in 10 predicts they will never retire."*
>
> Lydia Dallett

And, herein lies the problem for Millennials: Baby Boomers are sticking around for a while. They are hardworking and determined. As a result, they are the types of employees that companies want.

Since this generation wants to retire in comfort and luxury, they keep working to save up more money. This means fewer jobs available to a large, incoming workforce. In other words, Millennials don't have as many opportunities available because the accepted definition of "retirement" is no longer the same or at the same time.

The economy hasn't been strong either. You already know this. While it seems to be making a comeback, it will take a few years to reach greater stability. Right now, the economy is still struggling and that affects the job market in many different ways.

One way is that employers are choosing to fill part-time positions instead of full-time. As you probably already know, a part-time job barely paid enough to keep gas in your car, in high school. Simply put, they just won't pay the bills. So, why is this happening?

- The economy is still lagging and that means companies don't have the money to hire full-time positions. Part-time saves them money in numerous ways. They don't have to pay for insurance, retirement, and other benefits. Part-timersrarely get paid vacation either. It is easier on the company's budget.

- Government regulations on businesses mean that hiring part-time is simply easier. Want an example of this? Just look at insurance reform. While the Affordable Care Act has largely been a good thing, getting more people insured than ever, it has had some negative effects.

- According to the Affordable Care Act, in most situations, companies that hire less than 50 full-time employees do not have to provide insurance to those workers. Instead of hiring full-time, many of the smaller businesses are choosing to hire part-timers so they do not have to pay a part of insurance premiums, which can be costly.

Our generation hit the job market right when the economy hit its worst years. That's unfortunate, I know, but it is what it is. The positive in this negative situation is that we've been around during a terrible period, which has allowed many of us to adapt, becoming more independent and entrepreneurial.

Finally, we have to talk about the negative images of Generation Y. Millennials have a certain reputation and it just plain sucks, for lack of a better word. Just consider some of the article and book headlines that have been floating around for a while:

"Generation Y Bother"

"Millennials: The New Office Moron"

"The Dumbest Generation: How the Digital Age Stupefies Young Americans and Jeopardizes Our Future"

Time Magazine even referred to Millennials as narcissistic.

It is true that, yes, people generally assume our generation is full of self-involved, selfish, lazy people who lack intelligence because they have depended on technology too much.

This is simply not true – well, not totally true. Millennials do rely on technology, but that is more a symptom of the time we grew up and live. Overcoming this problem regarding perception means learning how to use the technology to our advantage. Becoming indispensable means honing that skill and putting it to use both as we continue to earn active income and as we transition to passive income streams.

The "Me" Generation

For a very long time, Baby Boomers were considered the "Me" Generation because this was the first group of people to worry more about the self. However, these days, Millennials are getting referred to as the actual "Me" Generation more and more. In fact, a Time Magazine cover referred to them as the "Me Me Me Generation." (It appears Time Magazine has a serious problem with us!)

At first glance, this may seem like a bad thing. Our generation is again referred to as self-centered and self-involved. But, before you feel even worse about your chances, consider how this image is actually a good thing:

"'It's viewed as an extremely self-centered thing – and that's kind of the point!' says Tim Tieu, who has his own consulting firm just two years after graduating from college. 'If you're not self-centered in this way...if you don't create a LinkedIn profile to show off your skills or if you don't have that personal website talking about your side projects...then you are at a disadvantage.'" Cindy Perman

In other words, thinking about YOU, unapologetically actually has its advantages. Some individuals stuck in the mindset of the past may not want to hire you because they worry you will be too selfish, but you and our entire generation will be much more likely to ensure you are out there, put your best foot forward, and make yourself more hirable.

Why?

While many may view this generation in a negative light, we are also a generation of engagement because we have grown up connected to the world.

The Positive View

While Millennials have been negatively stereotyped by some, there are also incredibly positive views of our generation, including:

- A generation that is strong in self-reliance. A group of people who know how to take care of ourselves and who will rely on ourselves instead of constantly needing something from everyone else. Self-reliance is a positive aspect when companies are hiring new employees, so we have that going for us.

- Millennials are known for being much more willing to work together on projects instead of trying to do everything alone. Since we are in a generation that fully believes in partnerships, this opens even more employment opportunities for you

- Finally, one thing that is often considered a negative can also be a positive. While some people assume that since Millennials have largely depended on technology more than any other generation before us, others recognize this as an advantage. It is no secret that technology is here to stay. It is an absolute staple in any business. Therefore, anyone who is tech savvy will automatically have more to offer any prospective employer.

Millennials, overall, have had a hard time getting ahead for a few different reasons. Timing has been a big part of it, coming into the workforce when the economy was at its worst in decades – let's just call that some really bad luck – dealing with high unemployment rates, and constantly having to fight against negative stereotypes has been a near-constant problem.

Now, it is time to recognize that those issues do not have to be a concern for you. By knowing how to play up the positives, then you can actually find it easier to develop a career based on the paths we will talk about in this book. From now on, no more focusing on the negatives and lots more focusing on what you can do.

Next, we are going to discuss a very exciting topic: how you can develop financial freedom through cash flow for "The New Retirement". That's the first step toward the financially independent lifestyle that you want.

Chapter Two:

Why Financial Freedom Through Cash Flow AKA "The New Retirement"?

Let me ask you something. Which would you rather do?

Work at a job 40-50 hours a week for many, many years and just barely get anywhere.

OR

Enjoy "The New Retirement" and become financially free at a younger age.

I am pretty sure the answer to that question is obvious. In fact, you probably would have given me a funny look if you could see me. "Did you seriously just ask me that?" That's probably what you are thinking. Of course, you want to become financially independent as soon as possible. Who doesn't?

That's why you want to learn how to use financial freedom through cash flow. That's the basis for "The New Retirement". But that may not be enough to explain why this is such a good thing, so let's go over some benefits to it.

The Problem with Current Theories

One of the biggest reasons why I really think people, especially Millennials, should consider this new method of retirement (aside from the fact that it is super cool) would be that you just cannot depend on current methods of retiring. Right now, many are probably assuming they will have a 401K or Social Security check to help pay for things when retirement finally arrives. But there are some problems with this.

- Social Security is already hurting due to various reasons, including the increase in demand for the benefit thanks to a rising population. Not to mention all the companies and local governments setting their systems up so as NOT to pay in to Social Security. How can it survive if something isn't done? The reality is simple: it can't. In the future, there is a good chance it will either go bankrupt or change to the point that it just will not be there to provide for all of our needs. We simply cannot put our retirement in the hands of something that is already severely in debt.

- The economy is never, in any way, predictable. We have seen this even in our own lifetime. It can go up on a whim, but it can also go down on a whim too. If you have your retirement funds invested with traditional 401Ks, then you could lose everything with one bad day on the stock market.

- Jobs are never guaranteed. Employees are not irreplaceable. Companies close. They downsize. They replace. If ever too comfortable in that traditional job, then you could be making a huge mistake.

Quit assuming that the traditional methods work. They don't anymore. As a part of this new generation, we have a chance to change things for ourselves. That's why this new retirement method is important to learn for the here and now.

Goal-Based

Have you ever tried to do something without a goal? Maybe you tried to lose weight, but you had no idea how much weight you wanted to drop. How much harder was it to accomplish? It is nearly impossible. Seriously, not having a goal can set you up for failure, no matter how hard you work.

Why?

Well, it's simple. Imagine you are walking down a path in a forest or on a sidewalk in the city if that works better for you. You are supposed to be getting somewhere, but you don't know where it is. How are you going to make the right turns or choose the right forks in the road? You won't. Instead, you are just going to keep wandering. And wandering. And wandering.

The same goes for your money. If you don't have a goal, you will wander. That won't get you anywhere. This is the first great thing about "The New Retirement" – it is goal-oriented. That means no more wandering. No more wondering which way to go. You will have a direct path to where you want to be.

25

Following these choices to financial freedom gives you clear and actionable goals. Here's an example:

> *Imagine you have $3,000 in monthly expenses after you pay off all your debt. This would mean you need $3,000 in monthly cash flow (the amount of money you have coming in after debts) in order to be financially free.*

This gives you a clear picture of what you need to do instead of offering hazy advice like "you need to make sure you are making money."

A Plethora of Options

Here's another great advantage – "The New Retirement" gives you options. I don't know about you, but I like knowing I have choices. If someone tells me "this is your only choice. You follow this or you don't do it at all," then I am not going to be very happy. If you are the same way, then you will love the fact that you do get to choose. Here are just some of those options you will get to pick from. Don't worry. We are going to go over these in detail later. This is just a brief introduction.

Market Investments

You know these better as things like:

- Stocks
- Bonds
- Mutual Funds

Market investments go beyond just a few options too. Many people find this fun and even entertaining. But there are also plenty of people who find it more than a little stressful. We'll talk about figuring that out for yourself a little later.

Real Estate

Real Estate has been a hot market for a while, looking for a way to invest in tangible assets. When the housing market is booming, it's pretty obvious, but sometimes people overlook it when things slow down. Say you are ready for this just when another real estate bubble has burst. Does that mean you shouldn't invest?

Anything can burst at any time. And while you do have to be more careful with Real Estate, keep in mind that they aren't making more land. There are different ways you can invest in Real Estate too:

- Single Family Homes (Purchase and Rent Out or Flip for a Profit)

- Multi-Family Homes (Like Apartment Buildings, Duplexes, and Condos)

- Commercial Property (Retail Stores and Other Businesses)

We will talk all about Real Estate investing, but keep in mind that if you like a tangible asset and stocks scare you a little, this could be a better route to choose.

Online/eCommerce

Thanks to all that technology we understand as Millennials, we have another method to build up that cash flow: the Internet. Online opportunities are virtually everywhere (see what I did there?). This is probably one of the quickest ways to get started bringing in the cash.

With the Internet too, you are hardly limited because there are so many different opportunities:

- Niche Affiliate Sites

- Blogging

- Podcasting

- Selling Products and Services

- eBooks

- Etc.

You probably already have a good idea what those things are – you are a tech savvy Millennial, after all. But, don't worry. We are going to talk about them in more detail.

Cash Flow Is King

Okay, I have mentioned it a few times – cash flow. It sounds pretty simple, right? It's the amount of cash flowing into your bank account. However, it's much more than this, so before you think you have it all figured out, let's decide what cash flow actually is.

Here's the technical definition from Investopedia:

> *"A revenue or expense stream that changes a cash account over a given period. Cash inflows usually arise from one of three activities – financing, operations, or investing – although this also occurs as a result of donations or gifts in the case of personal finance. Cash outflows result from expenses or investments. This holds true in both business and personal finance."*

Yeah, but what does that mean in real terms? I know that's what you are thinking. So, here's what you need to know:

- Cash flow refers to money that is coming into your account and then traveling out again if needed for expenses.

- Cash inflow is everything that you make. That can include work income, investment income, gifts, retirement, etc.

- Cash outflow is everything that you have to pay, including bills, debts, and everyday expenses.

Why does all this matter so much? Well, to put it simply: cash flow is king. Cash flow is the most important thing to know and have when it comes to retiring when you want instead of when you have to or are expected to. Cash flow matters more than anything else.

Of course, then you are probably thinking "well, I will have retirement, so I don't have to worry about all this." And, if that is what you are thinking, I have two things for you to think about:

- Do you really want to wait until you are pushing 70 to retire? At that point, you won't have much of a life left to enjoy retirement.

- Do you want to depend on money that doesn't come in everyday even though you have expenses every day?

That probably helped answer your question to some extent. But let me explain it a little further.

Social Security, Pensions, and Annuities

When most people retire they are in their 60s (or older) and depend on Social Security checks, pensions, or annuities to pay their expenses. A few problems come up with this.

All of these payments are based on monthly, quarterly, semi-annual, or annual cash disbursements. As a result, this has a big impact on cash flow. How can you ever build up regular cash flow when you are trying to live on payments that only come in once every few months?

Let's revisit the Social Security problem for a minute, shall we? Social Security – it's something that you can't ignore. You are most likely paying into it now, but no, you are not fully guaranteed to have it available when you reach retirement age, especially the way things are going.

U.S. News and World Report even included an article on this topic:

> *"According to the Social Security Board of Trustees, the system is already running a deficit, paying more in benefits than it's taking in from the payroll tax.*
> *Many 20-somethings never expect to collect any Social Security when they retire. Even middle-age workers doubt they will get their fair share of benefits. Social Security Expert Lawrence Kotlikoff, an economics professor at Boston University, warns 'People 50 and below should change their planning now to incorporate a benefit cut.'"* Tom Sightings

To some degree, the Baby Boomers are once again partly responsible for this trend, but don't be too hard on them. With such a large group of people hitting the "normal" retirement age at one time, they are making use of benefits as much as they can partially because they too are afraid of missing out on benefits and because they have reached the age where they simply aren't working anymore and need to use the benefits.

It should work out that the money someone puts in is available when they get older, but something here has not gone quite right. Somehow, not as much new money is being added in to the Social Security system, thus meaning less and less will be available later. There is great debate about how to fix this problem, including just eliminating Social Security altogether. That is not a debate I wish to take on, other than to make you aware of the problem that just keeps getting bigger.

What's that mean for you?

It is simple. There is great doubt as to whether or not Social Security will even be available when you want to retire. In that light, why would you want to take the risk when you have a much better option available to you.

Fact is, there isn't only one way to retirement, but the traditional path is in danger of not working for us in the long run and it surely doesn't help us in the short term.

Then,

> *Why wait to retire until you have lived most of your life?*

> *Wouldn't you rather retire when you are young and can do things you enjoy?*

> *Do you really want to depend on retirement money that may or may not even be available?*

Now, let me ask you the same question that started this chapter:

> *Why would you want to gain financial freedom through "The New Retirement"?*

I hope the answer to that question is much more obvious now.

Why would you want to do anything else?

You have an opportunity here. Don't be afraid to take advantage of it. You could change your finances right now and build true financial freedom well beyond what you imagined and well before you are 70 years old.

Now, we need to talk about the process and how this works. After all, you are probably itching to jump at the idea now. Why not? Why shouldn't you jump in? It's your chance to avoid the "normal" life you have been told by your parents and grandparents makes the most sense.

But slow down. Read through all the options in the book before making decisions so you don't end up sinking in the deep end.

I want you to succeed. I want you to enjoy your new retirement. Take your time as you take action – do it right, setting yourself up for life.

Over the next chapters, I will break everything down into the following four steps:

1. The Budget
2. Pay Down Debt to ZERO
3. Determine Your Passion (Or Desired Cash Flow Investment)
4. Start Investing

I will then break down each of the types of investment opportunities so you have all the information you need to build cash flow and enjoy the new retirement.

Chapter Three

What exactly is The New Retirement and what is it all about? Before we get into the process, let me make two things perfectly clear:

- It does take work. Money isn't going to just fall into your lap. But, I can assure you it will be a lot easier than the "normal" approach to retirement.

- You are going to have to be willing to do that work. Investing, purchasing real estate, building an online business – all of these things do need your attention, especially at the beginning.

I don't want to scare you away. I just want to make sure you know it won't be something that just happens without you lifting even a finger. But, it sure is easier than the traditional methods of working to retirement. This gives us Millennials a chance to actually enjoy life instead of breaking our backs until we have lived most of our lives and only be able to enjoy retirement when we barely can enjoy it at all.

This is what "The New Retirement" is all about. It is your answer to the question you weren't yet aware was nagging you. It is a secret to success that can be used by Millennials – or anyone else for that matter.

Are you ready to delve into the process?

The Budget

It's time to put together a budget. You can write out your budget by hand if you want to feel a bit old fashioned or you can do it on the computer. You can also follow the handy chart listed below to get your money in order.

It's easiest to do your budget on a monthly basis, but if you really want to drill things down, then you could budget your money weekly or daily, which could be important for avoiding unnecessary expenditures.

Before I get to the chart, here are some things you need to remember about your budget:

- Always leave room in your budget so that you never end up overspending. It doesn't matter what you expect to spend. Things could come up. You may spend a night out on the down barhopping with your friends. You may have to get your car fixed. No matter the issue, always leave space in your budget for whatever may come up.

- It's easy to overlook little expenses because you don't even think about them. But, they do add up. Let's say you spend $3 every morning for your Starbucks. You may not have thought to budget it, but that adds up to close to $100 a month. You have to budget everything.

- Your budget shouldn't be so strict you could never actually follow it. Leave money for groceries. Make sure you have money for your social life.

- The whole purpose of your budget is to get current debts paid off, so don't just factor in minimum payments. You have to pay more than that if you want to get out of debt.

Now, with all that in mind, let's make your life easier. On the next page is a chart anyone can use to make a budget. Feel free to copy it and customize it however you need based on your own situation.

A chart like this can accomplish a few things for you. It will help you start budgeting on a regular basis. However, it will also ensure you are paying attention to how much you should be spending compared to how much you are actually spending.

It also keeps you accountable. When you see those numbers on paper or computer instead of just figuring them in your head, you have no choice but to pay more attention to them.

This certainly helps me stay accountable for what I am spending.

Income/Expenses	Budgeted Amount	Actual Amount
Net Income source 1		
Net Income, other sources		
Fixed Expenses:		
Rent or Mortgage		
Insurance		
Car Payment		
Loan Payments		
Property Taxes		
Other		
Variable Expenses:		
Credit Cards		
Food		
Clothing		
Entertainment		
Fuel		
Electricity		
Water		
Phone		
Other Utilities		
Medical Bills		
Other		
Savings:		
Savings Account		
Emergency Fund		
Retirement		
Other		

Budgeting isn't always easy, especially if you have never done it before. I'm not going to sugarcoat anything for you. Right now, we need to go over the 12 most commonly made budgeting mistakes. I'm giving you a leg up so you can avoid making them. It will save you time and potential grief.

Mistake One: Having Unrealistic Expectations

It's pretty easy to get a little (or a lot) unrealistic about what you expect from your budget. You may have lofty dreams, but in reality, you do have to live. You have to have food to eat, clothes to wear, and a place to live. If you are so unrealistic about how much money you have to spend, you are going to put yourself in a bind and the whole budget will fall apart pretty quickly.

Mistake Two: Using the Wrong Tools

A budget is a budget is a budget, right?

Wrong.

Everyone is different, with different bills and expenses. You can't just use one budget and expect it to work because it worked for someone else. Even the template I provided won't work for everyone, but it is a place to start. You have to customize and make it your own.

Don't use a budget meant for someone else and expect it to work for you. Know you are different and your needs are unique. Build a budget that works for you in your situation.

Mistake Three: Not Having an Emergency Fund

We are going to talk about that emergency fund in depth. For now, just keep in mind that you need emergency money.

Life is unpredictable.

You could lose your job.

You could get sick.

You could be in a car wreck.

You need to make sure that you have money available if something bad were to happen. Of course, you hope it never does, but in reality, you have to be prepared.

Mistake Four: Not Creating Rules

We all need rules. When you were in kindergarten, the rules were things like walking on the right side of the hall or raising your hand before asking a question. In your adult life, the rules are different, but they still matter.

Now, you need rules about budget and money. If you don't have any, then you won't have anything to follow. You will just wander around, spending money as you want. You won't be able to follow the budget.

You need rules and you need to follow them for this to work.

Mistake Five: Not Being Able to Differentiate between Need and Want

This is a big one – one our generation has trouble with. We don't always know when we actually need something and when we just want it. The problem: if you get confused, you end up spending money that could have been used for better purposes. You have to get it clear in your head the difference between a need and a want.

- A need is something you have to have to survive: food, water, healthcare, transportation, clothes to wear, etc.

- A want is something that you would enjoy having but that you could actually survive without.

That's hard to do sometimes. I have stood in front of a big screen television and thought "I absolutely need this or I won't survive."

I get it. It won't always be easy.

To help you get a real idea of the difference between needs and wants, take a look at this chart that breaks it down for you.

Need	Want
Clothes	High-end couture clothing
Vehicle	Sports car with all the extras
Place to live	Custom built with swimming pool and golf course views
Meal	$100 lobster dinner from the fanciest restaurant
Water	$5 dollar bottles of high-end water that the celebrities drink

From now on, you have to know the difference between a need and a want so that all those wants you mistook for needs won't get in the way of staying on budget.

Mistake Six: Borrowing from Tomorrow

Have you ever heard the following phrase?

"Robbing Peter to Pay Paul"

It's a bit old, but you probably have heard it at some point in your life. It's a big problem when it comes to your budget.

In this scenario, Peter is your future. Paul is the right now.

If you keep borrowing from tomorrow to pay right now, you will never have that financially free future. It just doesn't work. Once you create a budget, you absolutely must stick to it. No matter what. Don't tell yourself: "Ok, I am going to borrow from next week's budget to get this thing now."

No. That doesn't work. You simply can't do that anymore.

Whatever you set for your budget this week, follow that. Run out of money? Oh well. That's just how it is sometimes. You may have to sacrifice something you want.

Mistake Seven: Being House Poor

You know that investing in property is a good thing so you decide to go look at houses. You go on a treasure hunt of sorts. It is exciting. You get to walk through all of these different homes. And then, you get to pick one for you.

Here's the problem. You may get approved for a $150,000 home loan. But just because a mortgage company says they will give you that much it doesn't mean you can afford it.

If you buy a house that is more than you can feasibly afford each month, then you will be house poor. In other words, you spend so much money on your monthly house payment, escrow, and insurance that you can't afford to do anything else.

In reality, it is best to actually spend less than you can afford. There's a reason for this. If you spend less than you can afford, then you have some leeway. Gas prices go up. The cost of living goes up. You may have an accident. In those situations, by spending less than you can afford, you have enough of a cushion to get through those tougher times.

Mistake Eight: Being Cash Poor

On a similar note, it is possible to be cash poor. That means you budget so strictly and are putting all of your spending money aside in a way that you have nothing left to deal with day-to-day incidentals.

Yes, you have to pay off bills before you can become financially free.

Yes, you need to be putting away six months of income (more on that later).

But at the same time, don't budget away every single cent. If you do, then you become cash poor. That actually puts you in a bad situation should something come up that requires cash money on the spot.

Mistake Nine: Buying on Credit

This is a big no-way, no-how.

Uh-uh. Don't do it. Nope. Nada.

If you buy on credit, then you are completely ruining your financial freedom. You are just making things worse. Don't, just don't. No more credit. It hurts you. It doesn't help you.

Mistake Ten: No Long Term Emergency Fund

This takes having a little emergency fund to a bigger level. If you don't have anything setback for the long term, what is going to happen if you are temporarily disabled, you lose your job, or something worse? All of your hard work would have been for naught.

Mistake Eleven: Not Talking It Out

If you have a spouse or a significant other, then you should be talking out the budget with them. If you are on your own, you should still be talking it out with yourself.

Every month, plan a meeting either with yourself or your partner. Then, go over the last month. Ask these questions:

- How did the budget go?

- Was it too strict or too lenient?

- Are there changes that need to be made?

- Are you happy with the budget how it is?

- Are we making progress toward financial freedom?

- Did we make headway paying off debts?

Go over all of the finances and make sure everything is happening the way you want it to. Then, make any alterations that may be needed.

Mistake Twelve: Spreading It Too Thin

This goes along with the very first mistake. If you are unrealistic about what you can and cannot accomplish, then you are probably going to have serious problems.

Here's the reality. There is only so much of you. There is only so much money.

If you spread it all too thin, something is going to give.

Avoid these mistakes, and you will find that it is much, much easier to set up a budget that is going to actually help you accomplish financial freedom.

Six Months of Income

For your budget, you absolutely must be putting 10% of your income into savings until you have six months of living expenses saved up. This will help protect you from unexpected circumstances.

I know, I know. You don't want to think about it. But, what happens if you lose your home, your income, or your health? You will need to survive for a while until you get things back in order. Having six months of expenses saved up, you will be able to get through these things.

Right now, you're thinking:

> *What if I don't have 10% to put into savings?*

There is no exception to this reality, you will need to find it.

You could cut down on some extraneous expenses such as entertainment, clothes, cable, or other things if need be. At this point, you also may need to pay the minimums on your debt to build this fund up. That's okay for the time being. Gettin that money saved up is the number one priority.

Pushing Your Debt

Once you have the six months of expenses saved up, then take that same 10% and start pushing it toward your debt to get things paid off. Some people may get their savings build up and immediately assume they are free to do what they want with that extra money. Don't be so impatient. Instead, use that extra money to pay down your debt.

We will cover this in more detail in the next chapter, you won't have to figure things out on your own.

Your Budget as a Guide

It's time to really get used to a budget because it is helpful in many ways. Even after you get all of your finances in order, your budget is still your friend. It keeps you from making mistakes with your money, and it is a good litmus test to see if you are financially free or not.

Now that we have all of that lined up, you know you need a budget and that you need to stick to it. After all, it will help you pay down your debt. That is one of your goals, right?

So what's next?

The next part of the process involves paying down that debt to ZERO, yes $0.

It is possible and it is a huge and necessary step toward achieving financial freedom.

Chapter Four:

Step Two: Pay Down Debt to ZERO

Debt is like a ball and chain hooked to your ankle. You always feel like you are dragging it around.

> *You want to go out to a club or even a nice dinner with friends but you know you shouldn't be spending money because of that debt.*

> *You want to go to a movie and all you can think about is that credit card bill.*

> *You see an awesome outfit, but you have an upcoming car payment you just can't pay without scrimping and saving.*

How is that possibly any good way to live?

The problem is, most of us Millennials ended up with a lot of debt from the get-go. We have tried to be independent and have ended up with student loans, car payments, credit cards, etc. And, if you aren't lucky enough to have a rich mom and dad, well then you have to deal with all those debts on your own. Of course, if you didn't have any debt, I doubt you would be reading this book in the first place, right?

Not to worry, though. Paying down your debt is actually easier than you think. Assuming you have saved up that six months of expenses, you are now ready to start eliminating that debt.

Believe in the Idea

Here's a little secret: when you don't believe in something, you can actually create your own future. Let's say you really want to lose weight. But, you keep telling yourself "I will never lose weight because I never have before." What do you think will happen?

Well, you aren't going to lose weight.

That's because when you convince yourself it won't happen, it never will.

That means it's time to become a believer in yourself. It is time that you believe you can actually get rid of every bit of your debt.

Here is the best part:

When you pay off your debt, and I mean pay it off in full, you will be bringing in money that you do not have to allot to those expenses.

That means, then, that you are essentially paying yourself. You won't have debt anymore. You won't be spending that money. It's like a really nice paycheck going directly to you.

Here's a simple version of that. Let's say right now you have a house payment of $1,200 a month. That's a debt because you don't actually own the house until you pay it all off. When you pay off that debt, suddenly you are paying yourself $1,200 a month.

That sounds pretty good, doesn't it?

The Debt Snowball

Dave Ramsey is known for his debt repayment plans, includingthe debt snowball – an effective method for eliminating debt. There's actually two different ways you can use the debt snowball. Let's look at both of them so you can decide what is best for you: Lowest Bill First and Highest Interest First.

Don't forget that you have to approach this with enthusiasm. And I mean real enthusiasm. You need to approach paying off your debt with gusto and determination to actually get it done. Keep reminding yourself of how great it will be when you don't have to pay anymore. Go all in, knowing it is going to change your life forever.

Lowest Bill First

In this first snowball method, don't worry about interest rates. Instead, list your debts based on how much you owe. Here is a basic scenario of debts that you may have:

Debt	Minimum Payment
$600 Store Credit Card	$45
$2,000 MasterCard	$100
$6,000 Car Loan	$125
$12,000 Student Loans	$115
$80,000 Townhome Mortgage	$700

Now, pay the minimums on everything except the smallest debt. In this case, it would be the store credit card. Put every spare cent you have into that debt. You could cut out some extraneous expenses. You could take on a part time job. No matter what it is, let's say you could pay $200 extra toward it plus the original $45.

Once you have it paid off, guess what? You move on to the next lowest debt, the MasterCard. Here is where it gets really exciting, you will have the $200 extra, the $45 you are no longer paying on the store card, and the original $100 minimum payment you were already making.

Instead of paying just the $100 on the MasterCard, you will be paying $345. Then, when you get it paid off, you move on to the car loan. And the whole thing just snowballs, building in size after each debt has been paid off. By the time you get to the car loan, you can feasibly be paying:

- The original $125 on the car loan.
- $45 from the store card.
- $200 you found extra in the beginning.
- $100 minimum payment from the MasterCard.

At this time, you aren't just paying the $125 car loan. You will be paying $470. As you get to the more expensive bills, you will have much more money available to pay toward them.

It's like kicking debt out the door one at a time. Soon, you have everything paid off, even your home.

Dave Ramsey reminds us, that there's another great thing about using this method. It should be relatively easy to eliminate that small debt. And, when you do, you will feel like you actually accomplished something. That will feel great. It will give you a reason to move on to the next debt, and then next one, until you owe zero.

Here's the second way to use Dave Ramsey's Debt Snowball Method. This time, list all your debts by interest rate with highest first. It may look something like this:

Debt	Interest Rate
$600 Store Credit Card	32%
$1,000 MasterCard	28.75% (Variable)
$12,000 Student Loans	8%
$6,000 Car Loan	5%
$80,000 Townhome	4%

This time, you are going to use the same snowball method, but you will start with the debt assigned the highest interest rate first. There's actually a couple of advantages to it.

The higher interest rates mean you pay more (due to fees) that you didn't actually owe in the first place. The longer you keep paying the minimums, you are just racking up hundreds or even thousands of dollars that goes straight into your creditor's coffers. It only makes sense to get rid of those highest interest rates first. You can save a lot of money and just like the first snowball method you just add your available money to start paying on the next debt as you get one paid off, then another and another.

Either one of these methods will work, but I personally recommend starting with the smallest debt and paying that off first. Here's why:

- Everyone likes feeling good about themselves, so when you are able to pay something off pretty quickly, then you will feel good about yourself.

- It's a great motivator and let's face it, we all need motivation sometimes. When you know you can actually make a big step and get something paid off, it feels good and gives you a reason to keep going to the next.

- You will make a lot of headway. While you may be saving the largest debt for last, you can get two, three, four, or even five debts paid off relatively quickly. Then, all of a sudden, you are able to pay large amounts on that last and biggest debt.

It works and it will work for you. Try it. Give it some time. Watch yourself getting closer and closer to financial freedom with each passing day.

Pay Off All Debts

I can't stress this enough. You have to pay off every single one of your debts. If you have one thing weighing you down, no matter how big or small it may be, then you still aren't financially free, now are you? Your debts include everything you owe money on. Some examples:

- Student Loans

- Car Payments

- Mortgages

- Personal Loans

- Second Mortgages

- Major Credit Cards

- Store or Gasoline Credit Cards

- Investment Properties

- Medical Bills

- Vehicle Repair Bills

The list could go on, but you need to make sure you think of every single debt you owe and pay each month.

Of course, this doesn't include certain recurring expenses like utilities, cell phone bills, insurance, etc. That's not debt. That's just living expenses. But, if you purchased on credit and thus owe anything, then it is debt and you need to pay it off ASAP.

Why is this so important?

You are reducing cash outflow. You are maintaining your inflow, but you don't have to pay a single thing out beyond day to day living expenses. And that is your ultimate goal – that's the key to financial freedom.

Again, like I have said before, let's say you owe $3,575 in monthly payments to debt holders. When you pay that off, you are switching your cash flow. All of that is coming in to you and not leaving.

It really is a big deal.

Reward Yourself

As humans, we are reward driven. I know that doesn't sound so great if you put too much thought into it. You are probably imagining a dog rolling over and high fiving to get a treat. It's much the same concept, but a little more sophisticated. It actually is a real thing that has to do with brain chemistry. When you accomplish something, your body releases "feel good" hormones. You feel great about what you have done, jubilant even. It's amazing! And when you reward yourself for what you have done, you will feel even better.

Now, here are some rules for rewarding yourself. (Yes, there are rules for this as well. Sorry!)

- Your reward absolutely cannot in any way put you back into debt. Do not put an expensive sofa or entertainment system on a credit card. Do not take out a loan to pay for a vacation. Just DON'T do it. You will be right back in debt if you do.

- Whatever way you decide to reward yourself, do so with cash. My favorite is an all-inclusive vacation that I pay for in cash up front. Why? Well, it is awesome. Have you ever been on an all-inclusive vacation? If you haven't then you are missing out. And, it is great because it will already be paid for. You won't owe anything and you can just enjoy it.

Let me tell you. It is absolutely refreshing to go on a vacation that is 100% paid off. You don't have to worry at all.

- Yes, there is such a thing as good debt and you may have heard about it, but even it doesn't belong in your life right now. When you are trying to become financially free, stay away from good debt as well.

  You cannot approach good debt (investment debt) until you have reached two criteria: you are financially free and you have excess passive income. If you don't have both, you have no business messing with good debt.

- Consider creating small rewards that won't harm your progress each time you pay off one debt. If you only reward yourself when you are totally complete, then you could lose your motivation pretty quickly. After all, your prize will be so far away it may feel unattainable. Absolutely save your big reward for the end of debt, but in the meantime, find some way to feel good with each debt you kick out the door.

Step two is all about debts and it is so important that you understand that getting out of debt has to be your main priority in the beginning.

Then, imagine getting to the end. You have paid off all of your debt. You book a hell of a vacation to the Caribbean. You paid for it in cash. You get to go on a cruise, sip Mai Tais, and know it is all paid off, just like you are.

Getting rid of every single debt you have is a huge step toward your early retirement.

Mistakes Made When Paying Down Debt

I really like to make things as actionable as possible. That's why I keep telling you stuff you can do, but just as important is stuff you shouldn't do. You can learn from the people who have come ahead of you. Learn from their mistakes and not make the same ones.

Here are the ten most common mistakes people make when they are paying down their debt.

Mistake One: Trying to Do It All Alone

You aren't superhuman. And you likely aren't a financial genius – who is? Quit trying to do everything on your own and assuming you have all the answers. It is okay to learn from other people and it is certainly acceptable to take advice from those that know more than you.

Obviously, you already have a bit of an inkling about this since you are reading this book and clearly want to learn. Learn from others when it comes to paying down debt, soak up any information you possibly can get, from anywhere reputable.

Mistake Two: Jumping into a "Debt Relief Program"

You have probably seen commercials or advertisements telling you how some company will help you pay off your debt quickly. It sounds like they are going to wave a magic wand and make your debts disappear with a *poof*. Too bad it doesn't work.

The "Debt Relief Programs" you may hear about often make things much worse. Some of them are downright scams. And, at the very least, they will damage your credit severely.

Don't get caught up with these programs. Instead, use the methods I have talked about here and pay down debt in a reasonable way, taking your time to get it done the right way for you and your life.

Mistake Three: Not Creating a Budget

I think I have said enough about this already to get the point across. If not, well then here it is one more time: YOU NEED A BUDGET! End of discussion.

Mistake Four: Tapping into Home Equity

It's a big temptation if you already have Real Estate. You could tap into a home equity line of credit, consolidate your credit card, and pay just one bill. Sounds great right?

Hold your horses.

The advantage of owning property is that you build up equity in it. If you sell that property, you will make a profit. You lose all of that if you take out a home equity line of credit. Doing this will put you further in debt and will take away your equity. It's just not worth it when you can methodically pay down your debt and still have the equity in your home.

Mistake Five: Not Following a Sensible Order

We talked extensively about how to create a sensible order for paying off your debt. There's a reason to do this. It will actually save you money. And it is the absolute best way to get out of your debt as quickly as possible.

If you don't follow a sensible order, then you are likely going to just keep throwing money at one debt or another and hoping something happens. It won't work. And, it will just slow down the whole process.

Mistake Six: Closing Accounts

Even though you will want to pay for things in cash from now on, it is very important to keep your credit score high. If you are investing in Real Estate, there may be a time when you do have to finance. That means you need to have a good credit score.

One mistake people make is closing each account or credit card whenever they get it paid off. However, that actually can damage your credit score. Having a few open accounts that are paid off will help. That's because you are showing you have the ability to pay for something should it come up.

Mistake Seven: Not Having an Emergency Fund

Again, I don't know how to reiterate this enough. You need six months of bills saved up for emergencies.

Mistake Eight: Staying with the Same Spending Habits

When you are trying to pay off debt, then you do have to change your spending habits. You don't get to keep everything the way it has been. After all, that's how you got in debt in the first place. Instead, you need to cut out some excess expenses so that you have more money to pay off debt.

If you have the biggest cable package, then cut it off. If you feel like you can't live without cable, then pare down to a smaller package.

Mistake Nine: Not Saving Anything

In addition to your emergency fund, you do need to save money as well. This savings can be the basis of investments later or it can be money that you just put away. When you are paying off debt, it is so easy to just throw everything you have at the bills.

You need to be saving money too. I know. That seems strange. But it really is important.

Mistake Ten: Not Checking Your Credit Report

Again, your credit report is important now and in the long run. You know technology, though. Chances are, as a Millennial, you have already had a run in or two with Internet scams and scam artists. Don't let someone ruin your credit through identity theft.

Be sure to check on your credit report regularly. And, you don't have to enroll in a costly program. Instead, you can check your credit report once a year for free from annualcreditreport.com (the only government approved site).

Take the time to do this as you pay down your debts. This will help you see what you have accomplished and it will help you make sure you aren't getting damaged by an identity thief. You can also monitor it regularly through free services like credit karma (www.creditkarma.com). The let you know of major changes to your score or inquiries. Be careful which sites you use. If they ask for a credit card number, then move on.

Now, let's move on to step three: determining your passion because you are going to build your positive cash flow out of something you love.

Chapter Five:

Step Three: Determine Your Passion (Or Desired Cash Flow Investment)

Let me tell you something. And, please hear me on this. If you don't listen to anything else, listen to this. You need to find your passion. Or, you at least need to find something you want to do for your cash flow investment. You can't pick something you hate. Believe me. It is very, VERY important that you get this.

Still don't believe me? Well, don't take my word for it. Here are a few reasons Siobhan Harmer tells us about why you need to find something you are passionate about:

- Working just for the money is not a good enough motivator to keep you going. If you have ever had a job you hate, then you know this. It can kill your soul. It can make you miserable, and suddenly, the money it provides doesn't matter so much anymore.

  When you actually care about what you are doing, then you have another reason to do it beyond earning money.

- When you find your passion, you will actually care about the work. You will approach it with more gusto. You will want to do it. You will feel accomplished when you do something.

- Quite simply, you will be better at the work too. That's because you actually like it and take pride in it. When you are better at it, you will get more done and you will move forward toward "The New Retirement" more quickly.

- Obstacles won't seem so bad anymore. If you hate what you are doing, then obstacles will seem huge. You will have a giant mountain standing in front of you and you won't have the right gear to climb it. When you actually like the work, that mountain will just be a molehill and you will be able to stomp it beneath your heel.

Now that we have established why you need to find your passion or something you want to do for cash flow investment. Let's talk a little about it. Go get a cup of coffee, pull up a comfy chair. We need to have a bit of a discussion.

Not Everyone Finds Investing Fun

You don't have to be like everyone else. If you don't think investing in Real Estate is fun, that's okay. It can be stressful. It can make you feel like you want to pull your hair out. You don't have to do the Real Estate thing.

Not everyone is willing to put the time and effort into an online business. After all, it does take a lot of work. It takes advertising, connecting, and using social media. It takes hours before everything becomes successful. And that may not be for you. If it isn't, that's okay. You have other options.

Many people just do not trust the stock market at all. After all, we have seen just how much damage that can do if something goes wrong. Again, that is okay if you don't want to use this method.

However, out of your different options, chances are you will find something that you find interesting or something you may even be passionate about. That is the thing YOU do – someone else won't think it is for them. That is just fine.

Do Research

How do you actually go about finding your passion? Just for humor sake, you could make a list, pin it to the wall, put on a blindfold, and then throw a dart to see where it lands. But, that's not something I would recommend. And seriously, it won't help you actually find your passion.

Instead, let's talk about research. Yes, you do have to research. No, it is not boring. It's fun!

I would recommend getting started with the research while you are paying off your debts in the previous step. In fact, I don't just recommend it, I would say it is a must. Here are a few different reasons:

- It will help you get a head start on figuring out which path you want to take.

- It's downright fun! While you are dealing with debt, looking into what you are going to start doing as soon as you are debt free is an exciting concept that will keep you entertained.

- It will get you ready for the next step, which will be heavy research to actually pin down your passion or your method of attaining "The New Retirement."

While you are paying off your debt, go ahead and look into all the things we will discuss here. You don't have to spend all your time doing it. Just get a preliminary idea of the things that peak your interest. This will help you throw out the ones that you know won't work for you and focus eventually on the ones that do get your attention.

Deeply Research Your Interests

Now, let's move on to when you have your debt paid off. You should have done all of the preliminary research and have narrowed down your interests to only a couple. It's time to kick things into high gear.

You really need to research the hell out of what you think you are interested in. And I mean research it until you have uncovered everything possible. Remember that what you choose is going to be for life – you need to love it for life.

Let's back up for a minute and discuss what is going to happen if you choose something and decide you don't like it later.

> *You basically pick something and go with it because you didn't do your research. At first, it seems interesting because it is something shiny and new. But, that shine wears off in a few weeks or months or years.*

> *Suddenly, you are back where you started from, doing something you really don't like every day. You start hating it. It certainly doesn't feel like retirement.*

Instead, you feel like you are trapped, yet again, with something you really don't like.

Does that sound like anything near what "The New Retirement" is supposed to be like?

Of course not. So, don't take that chance. Instead, take the time to do some pretty intense research and know just the right path that will work best for your life going forward.

When you KNOW exactly what you want to do, you will be ready to get started on it. But you have to make sure you TRULY know you are on the right path.

When you research your options, look at the pros and the cons. Consider the good and the bad before making a decision. We are going to explore those options further here too, so don't worry. You will get a head start by the time you finish this book.

Become a Sponge

Once you have pinned everything down and you know exactly which thing you want to pursue, then you need to become a sponge. And not one of those cheap sponges that just pushes water around. You need to be a really good sponge – one of those high quality ones you can get at Bed, Bath, and Beyond. Like a sponge soak up water, you can soak up information.

Learn everything you possibly can about the option you have chosen. Make sure you know it inside and out. Learn, and then when you think you know all there is to know, learn some more.

Use the Internet

The nice thing about the Internet is that it offers a plethora of free information. You don't have to spend a dime in the beginning. You can start your research here. That way, you won't spend any money while you are paying off debt.

Of course, too, when you are paying off debt, you don't need to spend money. If you do, then you are spending something that should have been put toward a debt.

Don't be afraid to use the Internet to its fullest extent. Learn everything you can for free.

Then, when you have exhausted your free resources (and finished paying off your debt), you can look into paying for more help.

Courses on the Subject

Once you are in a position to pay for learning more on the subject you have chosen, then you can actually enroll in courses. They are often available both online and in person.

Take the time to look around. You may find conventions and programs available right where you live or in a neighboring city. If that doesn't work out for you, then you can enroll in online classes. They are available from a number of different outlets.

A word of warning, however.

Some people are out to take your money without offering anything to you in return. You already know about the numerous different scammers out there, so it shouldn't be too hard for you to avoid them. Just verify whatever you are paying for and enrolling in is actually worth your while. Then, go for it and learn as much as you can.

Here's another thing about paid courses. Sometimes, they offer you a payment plan, which may seem great since it doesn't mean such an impact all at once. However, look at the fine print: you will probably be paying more money, even interest, and you will be going into debt yet again. That's the last thing you want to do.

Only enroll in paid courses when you have the money, pay up front, and save yourself some cash. This is a must-do.

Six Actions to Finding Your Passion

Okay, I have spent a lot of time encouraging you to find and follow your passion. But you may need a little help figuring out what yours is even if you have been doing research.

I want to end this chapter by giving you a little more information on how you can find your passion. Here are six actions you can take to guide your path.

Action One: Determine Your Talents

The best place to start is to consider your unique talents. What are things you just love? What are you good at? Don't feel like you are bragging. Instead, you are going over what you are capable of and what you are truly good at. Your passion is going to arise out of one of those things.

Write them down. Your list could look something like this:

I am good at being artistic and coming up with unique crafts.

I am good at talking to people.

I am good at understanding people's feelings and helping them get through bad times.

Your list could be virtually anything. Just take an inventory and know your own talents.

Action Two: Consider Who You Admire

Start thinking about people you admire. Chances are, something about them appeals to your passions as well. People who really love writing tend to admire authors. People who are passionate about numbers tend to admire mathematicians. Think seriously about who you admire and then consider exactly why you admire them in the first place. This action will provide serious insight into your inner desires and thus the passions that you can make your life pursuit without feeling like you are working.

Action Three: Remind Yourself What Mattered to You as a Child

When you were a child, you probably had certain things that you just loved. You probably even *knew* what you wanted to be when you grew up.

But then you grew up and forgot those things. It's time to go back to childhood. I don't care what it was you wanted to be. Just think about it.

Maybe you wanted to be a cowboy.

Maybe you wanted to be an artist.

Maybe your dream was to be a veterinarian.

No matter what it was, somewhere in all of those hopes and dreams of your childhood was a passion. Start exploring that more – and maybe your "New Retirement" will fall right into your lap.

Action Four: Fill in the Blanks

I am going to give you a sentence and all you have to do is finish it.

"If I had no chance of failure, no limitations, and I was guaranteed to be successful, I would..."

Finish that sentence. If you had nothing standing in your way, what would it be? What would you do? The answer is your passion.

Action Five: Know Your Compass

You have probably been ignoring your passions for a long time. When your mind and soul wanted to say "yes" you may have said "no" simply because it didn't seem right by the world's ridiculous standards. You forgot how to care about what you wanted because society said do this or that.

It is time to reconfigure your compass. If an activity comes along and you want to say yes, then there is probably good reason for this. That's because you may just have found your passion.

Action Six: Do What Feels Right

There are things in life that just feel right. They are usually easy. They don't require that much effort. They just seem to go with the flow. Ask yourself what things do feel right about and this will lead you on the right path toward your passion. There's a reason why it felt right in the first place – it is something that appealed to you on a deeper level. Knowing what feels right to you can help lead you to your passion.

Now, we have done all of the basics. All that's left is the final step: start investing.

Chapter Six:

Step Four: Start Investing!

Let's quickly recap what the process. At this point in the process, you will have:

- Put away six months' worth of living expenses and not touched that money.

- Paid off your debt (every single last cent of it).

- Pinpointed your passion or how you want to invest.

- Deeply researched your choice.

There is only one step left in the process: start investing.

For some inspiration, think about these words by Melchor Lim:

> *"Remember, every worthwhile venture in life intimate love, friendship, a new business, etc. is scary. These things are inherently risky. They are unsafe. These things aren't for the faint of heart. They take courage. And most importantly, they coexist with fear."*

If I sat here and said to you that you shouldn't be afraid, that would be unrealistic. You are going to be afraid. You are taking a big risk, albeit a calculated and smart one. Fear is a part of life – let it help guide you, rather than stop you.

You absolutely shouldn't allow paralyzing fear to win out. When you do, you will never start investing. Instead, recognize you are taking a chance, it is scary, and it is going to be amazing.

Believe in Yourself

I'm not going to get too new-agey. That would be a whole different book. Instead, what I am going to say is you do need to believe in yourself and your capability of enjoying "The New Retirement."

Look how far you have already come – you have cleared out the debt. You have chosen a passion. Now, all you have to do is take the leap and watch it completely change your life.

Ash Sweeney said:

> *"One of the reasons that many people don't live an extraordinary life is because they're too fearful to take a leap and believe in themselves."*

Ask yourself,

> *Do you want to be ordinary or extraordinary?*

> *Do you want to continue living the way you have been, just getting by, and knowing you will work until you are too old to enjoy much of anything?*

> *Do you want something better?*

Of course, you do. So don't let anything stand in the way of taking that leap.

Changing Your Life

Making the choice to start investing may seem like a big leap and it may be scary, but don't forget that it will truly change your life. You no longer have to live that life we so often refer to as "normal." You will be able to retire in comfort much sooner than you ever imagined. You will be able to do something you love. And you will love your life.

From here, there is only one direction you can go – and that direction is up. But to help you a little more, I am going to name the top five mistakes some people make when investing.

Top Five Mistakes People Make When Taking Action

People tend to make the same mistakes over and over again. You don't have to be one of those people. Instead, you can avoid those mistakes and move forward with confidence that you can invest in one of the methods I will talk about in the following chapters and start building your financial freedom.

Mistake One: Procrastination

Every moment you wait is money you are losing. Procrastination doesn't do anything. You could be missing out on valuable opportunities if you are not getting out there at just the right time. Don't take that chance.

Instead, get out there and get started. Now is the time. Waiting will not help you.

Mistake Two: Speculation

I have to be honest with you. Speculation – well it doesn't accomplish anything other than creating scenarios in your head. If you sit and wait and speculate, this is what you are going to do:

> *You are going to come up with every scenario that could go wrong. You will feed your fears. You will make up things that likely won't even work or happen.*

Speculation has no place in your life when you want to get out there and become financially free. Instead, do your research, take calculated risks, and just go out and do it.

Mistake Three: Over-leveraging

Leverage good investments through financing can be a good thing, but it can also be a problem if you overdo it. Leveraging too much can actual damage your portfolio. Use it sparingly and only when you really need to. Over-leveraging will just make things worse and create the wrong kind of risk – the risk of ending up back in debt.

Mistake Four: Not Asking Questions

You don't know everything. No one does. And I know you don't like that thought – who does? I don't like it when people tell me I don't know everything either. But it's a reality.

There is always someone who knows more.

There is always someone who is better.

Don't look at that as a bad thing. Instead, realize it is a good thing. Because there is someone else who knows more about a subject, you have an opportunity to learn. Whenever you get ready to invest, no matter which investment type you choose, always ask questions.

Get advice.

Learn.

Not asking questions is just being too prideful. Be willing to inquire of someone who may know more than you and you will be surprised at just how much more you will learn.

Mistake Five: Not Doing It

For whatever reason, if you aren't going out and getting it done, then you aren't getting anything done. Your biggest mistake would be not going through this process and becoming financially free.

You could keep on doing the same old thing – going to work, making active income, and just getting by. You could do that until you are about seventy. Then you could retire hoping you have enough money and live just a few more years realizing you didn't get to do the things you wanted.

Why?

Honestly, why would you do that when you have the chance right now to take action and become financially free? You could enjoy "The New Retirement" and love the results, love your life.

Don't make this mistake.

Instead, follow the idea that Nike had: "Just do it."

You will be happy with the results.

Now that we have gone through the process and you know the four steps to take to financial freedom, let's talk about the individual opportunities you could choose from. This will give you plenty of information and then you can pick the path, or paths, that interest you the most. Through further research, you will be able to narrow down to the right one for you.

Chapter Seven:

Types of Cash Flow Investments: Market Investments – Stocks

As I mentioned previously in this book, there are different types of cash flow investments. You do need to take each one of them into consideration. Make a promise to yourself right now that you will not use the blindfolded dart throwing method. It just won't work and guessing won't work either.

You need to be aware of all your options. The great thing is that you have plenty of opportunities from which to choose. You will be able to sift through all of them and find something that actually works in your life. Go into this section with an open mind.

Think you don't like stocks? Don't dismiss them until you have learned more about them.

Think you would be too overwhelmed by Real Estate? Don't let go of the idea until you have considered the pros and cons.

In other words, give it all a chance and then you will be able to choose the right option.

We are going to start right now with market investments. There is much more to this than just stocks too, so we will explore all of them individually in their own chapter. Market investments include: Stocks, Bonds, Mutual Funds, and Advanced Markets.

All of these have advantages, disadvantages, pros, and cons. You will need to consider everything before deciding if this would be a passion for you.

Market Investments

Let's jump right in and begin discussing market investments. We will start with stocks since they are most common and you likely already know a little about them.

Stocks

Let's get a clear definition of stocks to begin with so we are on the same page.

According to Investopedia,

> *"Plain and simple, stock is a share in the ownership of a company. Stock represents a claim on the company's assets and earnings. As you acquire more stock, your ownership stake in the company becomes greater. Whether you say shares, equity, or stock, it all means the same thing."*

Here's a simple way to look at it:

When a business is publically traded (publically owned and not owned by a private group or individual), then pieces of that company are owned by various individuals who have purchased stocks.

Exchange	Economy	City
New York Stock Exchange	United States	New York
NASDAQ	United States	New York
London Stock Exchange	United Kingdom	London
Japan Exchange Group	Japan	Tokyo
Shanghai Stock Exchange	China	Shanghai
Hong Kong Stock Exchange	Hong Kong	Hong Kong
Euronext	European Union	Amsterdam, Brussels, Lisbon, and Paris
Shenzhen Stock Exchange	China	Shenzhen
TMX Group	Canada	Toronto
Deutsche Borse	Germany	Frankfurt
Bombay Stock Exchange	India	Mumbai
National Stock Exchange	India	Mumbai
SIX Swiss Exchange	Switzerland	Zurich
Australian Securities Exchange	Australia	Sydney
Korea Exchange	South Korea	Seoul
OMX Nordic Exchange	Northern Europe Armenia	Stockholm
JSE Limited	South Africa	Johannesburg
BME Spanish Exchanges	Spain	Madrid
Taiwan Stock Exchange	Taiwan	Taipei
BM&F Bovespa	Brazil	Sao Paulo

If you invest in stocks, then you will likely do so in the United States with the New York Stock Exchange or the NASDAQ. However, for those who branch out to worldwide business stock options, then there are 20 major stock exchanges you need to be aware of, as indicated by the chart to the right.

For the purpose of this book, we aren't even going to touch on foreign exchanges. That's just more information that we can cover here. Instead, we will focus on American stocks.

In other words, when you invest, you will be investing in American businesses.

Overview of Stocks

Essentially, when you buy stocks in a company, you are part owner of that business. You have a very small claim in what the company owns. Obviously, if you bought more and more stocks in that business, then you have a larger and larger claim.

Investing in stocks doesn't just mean you own a part of the company. It also means:

> *You have a right to part of the company's earnings.*

> *You have voter rights in the company itself because this is attached to the stock.*

Once upon a time, when you purchased a stock, you got a certificate of ownership. It was fancy and covered in swirls along with elegant writing. You won't ever see those certificates anymore because a brokerage firm will hold onto them and the vast majority of what you do will be online.

Keep in mind that owning stock in a company doesn't mean you get to be the boss or anywhere near the boss. You own a small sliver of the profits. As the company does better, the price of stocks goes up and this gives you more money. You have a right to see those profits.

However, it doesn't give you the right to:

- Call up the CEO of the Apple Corporation and tell them what you expect to see in the next iPhone.

- Walk into a store and pick up a free case of Coors Light.

- Think that you will get free Toothpaste for life because you have stock in Proctor and Gamble.

By the way, just in case you are curious, those stock symbols would be AAPL, TAP, and PG respectively. Knowing the stock symbols is important to following the stocks in which you are invested, keeping up-to-date with how that stock is performing, which just happens to be easier than ever before, thanks to the Internet.

Once upon a time, knowing the value of stock meant watching a news channel and waiting for the symbol to come up at the bottom of the screen. These days, you can hop on the computer, type in the name of your company or the stock symbol through Google and you will immediately get an updated stock value, how much it is up or down, and even a chart where you can view its trends for a day, five days, a month, three months, a year, or even five years. That's a lot of information right at your fingertips.

Common and Preferred Stock

There are two essential types of stocks you could pick from. There is a lot of exciting material to learn about the stock exchange, beginning with common and preferred stocks.

- Common Stocks – These are, well, to put it simply, common. This is the type of stock you will hear the most about. They represent the type of ownership in a company or a claim on part of the profits. Investors in common stock get one vote per share in order to choose board members.

- Preferred Stocks – With preferred stock, you have some type of ownership in the company, but you don't have voting rights. Investors are usually on a set of fixed dividends for the whole time they own stocks.

There are advantages to preferred stocks, including the fixed dividends and that these shareholders are paid off first before any common stock shareholders. Of course, as you can imagine, there are difficulties with preferred stocks as well, so don't think they are the perfect option.

Now, as I mentioned dividends, I should probably explain them too.

Breakdown of Dividends

It's important that you understand dividends because this is a big part of stock investing. According to CNN Money, here is a simple definition:

> *"A dividend is a payout that some companies make to shareholders that reflects the company's earnings. Often paid out quarterly (every three months), dividends give stockholders a steady return, regardless of what happens to the stock price."*

Not all companies pay out dividends, so don't get so excited quite yet. Usually, this is something offered by well-established or older companies. Newer companies probably do not pay them. Keep in mind that even if you invest in stocks through a company that pays dividends, these are not guaranteed. If the company doesn't make a profit, you aren't going to get anything.

Reinvesting

There's a simple way you can use dividends to grow your money even more quickly. If you invest in a company that pays dividends, then you should turn around and reinvest any dividends you receive. If you keep the money, then yes, you have that cash, but you aren't doing anything with it. By reinvesting, you are giving yourself a chance to make more and more.

Buying Stocks

There are two main ways you can purchase stocks. The best thing you could possibly do would be to hire a professional financial planner. That's because an expert will know how to go about buying stocks, when to buy, and when to sell.

Let's talk about the two ways to buy stocks:

1. Brokerage – This is the most common option. Brokerages can be full service, which means they will provide you expert advice, will manage your account, and will handle everything for you. The other type, discount brokerages, will offer less attention and will require for you to be more hand's on, but they cost less money. There are pros and cons of each, so do your research on brokerage firms you are considering.

2. DIPs – This stands for direct investment plans. Some companies allow shareholders to purchase stocks directly from them. However, this is very rare and is not the path you would likely take.

If you have a financial planner, which I do recommend so you can enjoy your "New Retirement," then you won't have to worry about figuring out the best way to buy a stock. Instead, someone else will do all the heavy lifting for you.

Pros and Cons of Stocks

Now that you know a little (or a lot) more about stocks, you probably have one big question: what are their advantages or disadvantages? Obviously, before you take the leap and choose to invest for your method of increasing cash flow, you need to know the good, the bad, and the ugly… and I am not referring to that old Clint Eastwood spaghetti western.

The Pros

Let's look at the positives first because they are more fun, right? Here are all the advantages you would get from investing in this way.

- If you invest in companies with dividends, then you will get money every time they make a profit. Since these companies are large and well-established, they are also the most stable stocks.

- With dividends, then you will earn up to 6% or more of the company's profits depending on the number of stocks you own.

- Stocks give you a chance to get into something big before it gets big. Can you imagine if you had stock in Microsoft back when it was a little startup? When a company grows by leaps and bounds, that means the value of your stock will go up incrementally.

Yes, stocks can give you a big chance to make money in a couple of ways. Sounds pretty amazing, right? Well, let's look at the cons so that you can weigh them against each other and make the right decision for you.

The Cons

Of course there are negatives to any financial decision you make. It would be ridiculous to jump into anything without knowing all of the potential negatives too. So then, here are the cons:

- Markets are volatile. Something that has been doing great one day can take a nosedive the next and that means you could lose a lot of money. And even dividend stocks do not promise money.

- When companies are in dire straits, then they will often cut dividends. That means even if you buy into dividend stocks, that doesn't mean you will get anything.

- You actually have to be careful of companies with unrealistically high dividend yields. Keep the old adage in mind: if something seems too good to be true, then it's not true. This matters right here. A lot of times, companies will give out ridiculously high dividends when they are in trouble and if you aren't careful, you could be buying into a sinking ship.

Now, after we have talked about all of those details, I want to make it a little simpler.

When you buy a stock, you own part of the company and thus part of the profits and losses.

I know I already said that at the onset, but it really is all you need to know. You can make big money or lose big money. Let's see if I can help ensure you only face the former and not the latter.

I am going to give you some great insider advice. I know that the stock market can be difficult and if this is the path you choose to follow to financial freedom, then you are going to need everything possible on your side. I am not just going to list common mistakes made on the stock market – here I am going to list mistakes even the most qualified and experienced investors have made.

That way, you can avoid them and have a leg up, even over the very best.

Mistake One: Not Considering Value

It is easy to forget value when paying too much attention to favorites. Just because you really like a company doesn't mean that's the best option for investing in stocks. Don't worry so much about what you like and don't like. Instead, take the time to look into value, understand the stocks that do have the right value and choose them instead.

Mistake Two: Getting Too Arrogant

When you make some successful trades, you may find yourself getting too big for your britches. You feel comfortable and think you are good to go no matter what. The problem is, you can absolutely never get comfortable in the stock market.

Always stay on your toes.

Never get arrogant.

Only then can you avoid a very costly mistake.

Mistake Three: Not Diversifying

While stocks aren't exactly diverse in their own right, there are things you can do to avoid putting all of your eggs in one basket. Even if you choose to use only stocks as your investment option, then you need to avoid putting all your hope into one thing.

What do I mean?

Well, simply put: buy more than one type of stock.

One company could be doing fantastic right now, so you may think you should buy up as much stock as you can right there. What happens if the company goes under? It could happen at any time and we have seen it in our lifetime. The companies that seem to be doing well could fail at a snap of the fingers. In the same light, a company seemingly on the verge of failing could have that big break overnight.

You can never know what will happen, so even if a company looks great, you need stock in more than one place. That way, if one company fails, you won't lose everything.

Mistake Four: Thinking You Are Unique

You are special. Don't get me wrong. We all are. However, in the world of the stock market, you aren't. There are plenty of other people just like you. If you spend your time thinking you should get special advantages, you are doomed to mess up.

Instead, accept that even to your financial planner, you aren't anything special - just another investor. Be willing to work on investing without bias and you will get better results.

Mistake Five: Worrying Too Much About Yield

It is easy to do this when interest rates are low. You feel like you are paying substantially for something that would normally be lower. Since you are paying more, you think you should get more yield. However, you may actually have to give up some dividend income. While that's not the best outcome for your cash flow, it is the reality in a fickle market.

Be willing to worry more about smart investments and less about yield and this should result in long-term benefits.

Mistake Six: The Tax Issue

Taxes can be confusing. Taxes can lead you around like a bull with a ring through its nose. Because it can be so difficult to understand, the worst thing you could do is try to handle it all on your own.

Again, you need a financial planner. You need someone who understands taxes and will help you avoid getting crushed by the Capital Gains Tax.

Mistake Seven: Jumping Ship Too Soon

When it comes to your money and investing, you are going to get emotional. If the stocks falter, you are liable to get scared and worry that you need to jump ship. That isn't necessarily the best idea. Instead, take emotion out of it.

Be cold and calculating.

You need to consider whether or not there is a good chance the stock will bounce back. If the stock has potential, don't jump ship because of your emotions. Give it time and see what happens.

Mistake Eight: Rushing without the Research

I cannot tell you enough how important research actually is. You need to know exactly what you are doing before you do anything and that includes buying a stock. Do not buy anything until you have researched it. Know exactly what you are getting in to, what the company stands for, and you may just be okay.

Mistake Nine: Ignoring the Market

You really do have to pay attention to the market – all of it – even if you are invested in only a couple of companies. The whole market and what is going on with it will give you a good idea of what your stocks are going to do.

Don't just ignore the whole market because you are worrying about your stocks. Look at the big picture and keep up with everything. This is just a part of investing in this manner.

Mistake Ten: Worrying about the News

The news can definitely reel you in. You see things that scare you and you think you need to sell everything as soon as possible. However, the news is sensationalized. Paying attention to it is acting as an amateur. You need to worry about the market only because that is where your money is at.

Avoid these mistakes and you will actually have a leg up over even the more knowledgeable traders.

And once again, remember that owning stock means you own part of the company.

That's truly all there is to it. You own a part of the company. It may be a very small portion of that company, but it is yours. That gives you some type of rights in that company.

Bonds are different and that's why we are going to talk about them in a separate chapter next.

Chapter Eight

Types of Cash Flow Investments: Market Investments – Bonds

If stocks are the sexy model who you saw in the coffee shop, then bonds would be the sweet girl next door who has sex appeal, but doesn't get the same attention. As a result, when people hear about market investments, they don't always think about bonds, but they could be worth your attention if this is the route you choose.

The bad thing is, many people don't even know what a bond is. It's okay if you don't. There are a lot of people who don't. Let's start with an explanation before we jump into more about them.

Investopedia defines bonds in the following way:

> *"Just as people need money, so do companies and governments. A company needs funds to expand into new markets, while governments need money for everything from infrastructure to social programs. The problem large organizations run into is that they typically need far more money than the average bank can provide. The solution is to raise money by issuing bonds (or other debt instruments) to a public market.*
>
> *Thousands of investors then each lend a portion of the capital needed. Really, a bond is nothing more than a loan for which you are the lender. The organization that sells a bond is known as the issuer. You can think of a bond as an IOU given by a borrower (the issuer) to a lender (the investor)."*

So, in other words, bonds follow this progression:

A company or government needs money.

They write out IOUs and ask for money.

You can buy some of those IOUs. That means you are lending money.

You will receive interest based on a predetermined schedule.

The company will need to pay you back before the bond maturity date.

That's the basic definition.

Overview of Bonds

One thing that you need to understand is there is a big difference between stocks and bonds. Bonds are considered debt. That's because you do not have a tangible asset for your money. Stocks are considered equity because you are actually buying a portion of the company.

Here's something interesting too. When you buy a bond, you become the creditor. Someone owes you money. It could be a government or a business, but either way, they are in your debt. They have to pay you back by the bond maturity date

As a result, you will find that bonds are much less risky than stocks.

I know that may or may not appeal to you. Some people like the adrenaline rush that comes along with taking stock risks.

Some people don't.

If you don't like that risk, that doesn't mean you are a wuss. It just means you want to go a different path. And bonds could be right for you.

The Types of Bonds

Because there are different entities that can issue bonds, it only makes sense then that there are different types of bonds as well.

> Treasury Bonds – This covers any bonds that are issued by the United States Government. They also go by the names Treasury Notes, Treasury Bills, and T-Bills. This is considered the safest type of bonds you could purchase.

Municipal Bonds – These would be the next safest set of bonds because they are issued by cities. Local governments can create bonds that are actually tax free, but the yield will usually be lower.

Corporate Bonds – Next in the progression of risk would be corporate bonds. These are bonds issued by large corporations. Companies have a great deal of flexibility for issuing debt. These bonds will offer a higher yield, but they do include higher risk as well. There are two different types of corporate bonds too.

> Convertible Blonds – This is one of the two types of corporate bonds. They refer to bonds that you would actually be able to convert into stock if you so choose.

> Callable Bonds – These are the second types of corporate bonds. They allow the company to redeem the bond issue before it has reached maturity.

Zero Coupon Bonds – This final type of bond is unique. It doesn't issue coupon payments but offers a discount to par value. Essentially, you will know exactly what you are going to get when the bond matures in ten years. For example, if you buy a zero coupon bond with a value of $800 and you purchased it at $500, then when it matures, you know you will get exactly $800.

Of course, you will need to do a great deal more research into choosing the right type of bonds, especially when taking into consideration specifics about who is issuing the bond and why. Again, having a financial planner will help to ensure you make the right choices.

Bond Interest

Stocks often pay dividends and that is how traders can get extra income from their purchases. Bonds are a bit different. They don't pay dividends, but for the most part, they pay interest. Here's an example:

> *If a bond worth $100 has a 10% annual interest rate and a ten-year life, then you would get interest payments of $10 per year for ten years. At the end of the maturity, you would*

get the $10 for that year along with the original bond price of $10. Over the ten years you would end up making an extra $100 on that bond.

Not all types of bonds offer interest payments, including zero coupon and municipal, so keep that in mind if you choose to buy them.

Buying Bonds

If you want to buy bonds, then you will need to go through a full service or discount broker. You will likely need a minimum investment and you will need to pay the broker for their services.

If you would like to buy government bonds, then you have a couple of options:

- You can often buy government bonds through your bank. They often issue them so that you do not have to go through a broker.

- If your bank doesn't issue government bonds, then you do have another option. You can buy them directly from the United States Treasury by going to www.treasurydirect.gov. That way, you don't have to work with a broker.

Now, you probably know more than you ever thought you would about that attractive girl next door (I mean bonds) and you may have as much information as you did about that sexy model (I mean stocks).

But, we have one more thing to cover: the positives and the negatives. Once again, you have to know the good and the bad before you can make any decisions.

Pros and Cons of Bonds

We have already established that there are positives and negatives to anything you choose to do. And, that's true of bonds as well. Let's look at the pros and cons.

The Pros

There are plenty of great pros to bonds that may get your attention. But, hold up before you go in feet first. We will talk about the cons in a minute.

- Bonds are fairly safe. They offer you much less risk than stocks.

- Another sweet thing about bonds is that you will get regularly scheduled payments. That means a secondary source of income without having to do anything.

- When you buy a bond at a certain interest rate, then you get that interest rate no matter what, even if rates go down in the meantime. This is guaranteed by law.

- You can sell bonds before their maturity date. It may be more difficult than selling stocks, but you can do it, giving you an option if you want one.

Of course, the biggest advantage of bonds will always be that they are safer. You don't have to worry about the stock market crashing or a certain stock going down just because a company's new update didn't get quite the attention expected.

The Cons

Now, let's look at the negatives of bonds because you can't make an informed decision without seeing both sides of the story.

- Taxes can be on the higher side when it comes to bonds. The interest payments you receive from bonds will be taxed and they are taxed higher than any other investment you could choose. That's because the tax rate will be based on your income, not the bond itself.

- While bond interest stays the same even if interest rates go up, the same is true in reverse as well. If the interest rates go up, you are still stuck where you were when you bought the bond. You don't get more money.

- When it comes to taking less of a risk, it also means less of a reward. You won't make so much money with bonds. You know exactly what you are going to get, though, which appeals to many people. However, when you invest in something riskier like stocks, then you have the chance to make much more money.

- You won't get paid frequently. For the most part, you can expect bonds to pay twice a year, so it's not a regular source of income that you can depend on for a monthly basis. Additionally, if you buy zero-coupon bonds, then you won't get interest until the bond itself matures.

Weigh the pros and cons of bonds just as you would with any other type of market investment. They may be the right option for you, but then again they may not.

Let's summarize bonds in simple terms too:

With a bond, a company or government owes you.

You could think of it as the direct opposite of stocks. With stocks you are buying into the company, with bonds the company is borrowing from you.

In other words, it is like a loan. You are the lender and you will be paid back by a certain date.

Mistakes People Make with Bonds

Again, I want to help you out by going over the mistakes people make with bonds. Avoid the following mistakes and have a better time with bonds.

Mistake One: Brokers Don't Know Everything

When you are investing with anything on the market, you need a financial planner. For bonds, you should listen to expert advice, but at the same time, remember that your broker or planner doesn't know everything either. If you have researched something and you feel really strongly about it, then there is a reason why your instincts are speaking to you. Listen to them. Don't let your broker make all decisions for you without you knowing what is going on.

Mistake Two: Ignoring TRACE

Something that you need to be very familiar with when buying bonds is TRACE. That stands for Trade Reporting and Compliance Engine. It is designed to make sure everything with bonds is transparent. You should take the time to pay attention to it because it can provide you with a ton of valuable information.

Ignoring it and just doing whatever you want without knowledge will likely lead you in a bad direction.

Mistake Three: Looking Only at Short Term Performance

I know how easy it is. You want to look at the short term because that's what is tangible right now. A bond may get your attention because it is going to help you with cash flow in the next year. That kind of short term success will dazzle you.

But, let me ask you something:

> *Do you only want financial freedom for a year?*
>
> *Or*
>
> *Do you want financial freedom from now on?*

You should have chosen the latter of those two. And if you did, then you have to look at the long term performance of the bond, not just what it is doing right now.

Mistake Four: Not Looking at Expenses

There are always going to be management expenses to bonds. But, if we want a dose of reality here, we are going to have to accept that bonds don't necessarily bring in enough to warrant super high expenses.

You have to be careful of this. Before you buy any bond, you need to know what the management expenses will be and you also need to know if those expenses will be worth it based on the yield of the bond.

Mistake Five: Only Looking at High Yield Bonds

It is easy to get so dazzled by high yield bonds that you assume they are always the best options. It is a chance to make a lot of money, yes, so why wouldn't you want to take it? The problem is, if the economy suffers, then in many cases this can damage your bonds too.

Look at different types of bonds:

- Long-term

- Short-term

- Investment grade

- High yield

- Low yield

You need to mix things up and don't just let those flashy high yield bonds get all of the attention.

Mistake Six: Getting Too Complicated

There are some really confusing bonds out in the world and getting involved in them will leave you overwhelmed. It is always best to keep things simple. Watch out for those complicated bonds like:

- Reverse Convertible Bonds

- Catastrophe Bonds

- Leveraged Bonds

- Inverse Bond Exchange Traded Notes

- Floating Rate Bonds

They are complicated, and at least in the beginning, they don't have a place in your portfolio. If you want to get complicated later when you really know a lot more about investing, that's fine. But stay away from them in the beginning.

Mistake Seven: Ignoring Inflation

Inflation is really a problem and it can be a big issue when it comes to bonds. The best way to explain this is through an example:

> *Let's say you buy a bond with a 6% yield. That sounds pretty good.*
>
> *Inflation, however, will be 3% over the time frame of the bond.*
>
> *That means your yield is cut down to 3%.*
>
> *Then, you get taxed on the original 6% bond.*
>
> *What are you left with? Hardly anything.*

You absolutely have to calculate for inflation because bonds do have longer maturity dates. If you don't consider inflation as well as taxes, you could end up losing all of your profits.

Mistake Eight: Only Retiring on Bonds

Bonds are great, but they can't be the end all, be all. If you want to stay in market investing, go for it, but consider adding in other things like stocks or, if you are especially brave, advanced markets.

Bonds can help, but they don't make big leaps in cash flow. Use them, but use other things too.

Before you make a final judgment on market investments overall, let's talk about another option: mutual funds. These are different from stocks and bonds, so we need to spend some time looking at them separately in the next chapter.

Chapter Nine:

Types of Cash Flow Investments: Market Investments – Mutual Funds

There's another type of market investment you could choose. In a way, it is more like a subcategory. You may even know a little about mutual funds because they have been gaining popularity and attention over the last few decades. In fact, it really wasn't that long ago when mutual funds were pretty obscure, but throughout the life of the Millennial generation, they have been fairly popular.

What are mutual funds then? Just because you have heard of them definitely doesn't mean you know exactly what they are. They really aren't that hard to understand.

So then, let's begin with the Investopedia definition:

> *"A mutual fund is nothing more than a collection of stocks and/or bonds. You can think of a mutual fund as a company that brings together a group of people and invests their money in stocks, bonds, and other securities. Each investor owns shares, which represent a portion of the holdings of the fund."*

In laymen's terms: you buy a mutual fund and it is like having a whole group of stocks and bonds all in one place. It's the preferred method used by many "traditional retirement" planners because it is quicker and simpler than the alternative of buying individual stocks and bonds.

Overview of the Investment

Yes, mutual funds simplify your life,. But that isn't the only reason why people like them either. Another advantage is that mutual funds offer income in three different ways:

- You can receive income from the dividends on stocks and the interest on bonds. The mutual fund will pay throughout the year in distributions.

- If there are securities in the fund and they increase in price, you will actually get to enjoy a capital gain. That gain will be passed on to you and any other investors.

- When fund holdings increase in price and are not sold, then the shares increase in price too. You will have the opportunity to sell your shares and earn a profit.

As you can see, you have numerous opportunities to profit from mutual funds. And, you also have an option when it comes to what to do with your profits. You can receive the cash in the form of income or you can reinvest the money if you would like.

Different Types of Mutual Funds

There are a few different types of mutual funds and knowing more about them will help you understand what you should invest in if you take this path. It's important that you learn as much as you can so you can choose for yourself. Different mutual fund types have different goals,which may be going in one direction and you in another.

- Equity Funds – These mutual funds are made of stocks only. However, instead of buying the stocks individually, you get them in one batch.

- Fixed Income Funds – These mutual funds are made primarily of bonds. Again, you buy them in one batch instead of individually.

- Money Market Funds – These funds contain a few different things including US Treasury Bills, CDs, commercial paper, municipal notes, repurchase agreements, and federal funds.

Obviously, there is much more to the types of mutual funds than this and it does help to have a professional financial planner on your side helping you make total sense of them.

Now, just in case mutual funds still don't quite make sense to you, here's an easy way to look at it.

Imagine that mutual funds are a recipe, similar to a cake.

Recipe for a Cake:	**Recipe for a Mutual Fund:**
Eggs	Stocks
Flour	• Google
Milk	• Southwest Airlines
Vanilla Extract	• Twitter
Icing	Bonds
Candles	• 30- year
	• 5- year

See how they kind of look similar? When you think of mutual funds as a recipe all adding up to one fund for you just like all of those other ingredients create one single cake, then this is much easier to understand.

Interest and Dividends

As I already mentioned, one of the interesting things about mutual funds is that they combine the payout between dividends and interest. We already talked about both of them in a previous chapter, so there's no reason to go over it again.

Just keep in mind that when you invest in mutual funds that have dividend stocks and interest bearing bonds, then you will get two different types of payouts. And, that means more income.

Pros and Cons of Mutual Funds

At the moment, mutual funds sound pretty darn fabulous, don't they? Well, hold your horses and before you decide this is the way you want to go. It's a smart idea to weigh the pros against the cons. Because, yes, there are cons of this market investment and you need to know what they are before you do anything.

The Pros

You probably already have some idea of the pros that come along with mutual funds, but let's run them down so you can tick off the positives and then compare them to the negatives.

- You know the old phrase: "don't put all your eggs in one basket." That's because if you put all of them in one basket and you drop it, then you are going to have a bunch of broken eggs. One of the positives of mutual funds is this is a great way to quickly and easiley put eggs in different baskets.

  With mutual funds, you will have diversification. Your risk is spread out over several different types of things and that means less of a chance of losing it all.

- Transaction costs are lower. That's because these mutual funds buy and sell bigger amounts of securities, stocks, and bonds in one batch. You won't have to pay nearly as much for the transactions themselves.

- With mutual funds, you can sell at any time, which means they are highly liquid. This makes life much easier on you. Want to sell? Well, go for it. You can sell whenever you like. That's much different from other options.

And, of course, there's the simplicity of the whole thing. And, who doesn't like simplicity? With mutual funds, you can buy one thing and have a have a huge variety in your portfolio all at once. It's much, much simpler than having to buy and sell each individual stock or bond.

The Cons

Then there are the cons. Yes, there are bad things about mutual funds. There is good and bad with anything you could possibly do in life. And, if you ignore the negatives, you could get yourself into a big mess. So, let's look at the cons and then you can decide if mutual funds are right for you.

- While the cost of buying and selling mutual funds isn't so expensive, there are other costs involved. The very process of running and creating mutual funds is expensive and that cost will filter down to the investors. Each fund will have a different type of fee and when you are buying, you really have to pay attention to this. You don't want to buy a really expensive fund and waste a large amount of money that you will never get back.

- Mutual funds can get really diluted too. In other words, you can over-diversify. When you have money in too many different places, there is no one spot that has enough to bring you high returns. Dilution happens when a fund is successful and a ton of people want to invest in it. There isn't much to do with all that money and that means so much dilution that no one will make much money at all.

- Mutual funds tend to trigger the capital gains tax too. There are ways to handle this through tax sensitive funds or holding funds that aren't tax sensitive in a tax-deferred account, but for the most part, keep in mind that you will have to pay taxes on mutual funds or at least the income you get from it that is.

Once again you are left with a question. No, that question isn't "what is the meaning of life?" You will have to figure that one out on your own. The question here is whether or not mutual funds would be something for you to consider on your way to being a retired Millennial.

Mistakes People Make with Mutual Funds

Because so much can be going on with mutual funds at any given time, it is really easy to make mistakes. I just don't know how to tell you enough that you need to know what is going on with your investments. And you can help yourself by avoiding these common mutual fund mistakes.

Mistake One: Having No Idea What You Actually Own

If you have hired a financial planner, then good for you. You made a very wise decision. However, that doesn't mean you can rest on your laurels and never worry about your investments.

You absolutely need to know what is going on with your money.

Even though a mutual fund includes a lot of different things, you should know exactly what you're investing in.

What companies do you have stock in?

What types of bonds do you have?

How is your money split up?

These are the types of questions you should always know the answers to when you have money in mutual funds.

Mistake Two: Worrying too Much about Performance

Okay, well there are some areas of your life when you probably do want to worry completely about performance (wink, wink). But performances itself is not the end all and be all when it comes to mutual funds.

A fund may be really hot right now and you may be tempted to go after it. But you can't just consider what's happening in the moment. You have to think about the fund's long-term results. That's what matters when you are trying to build cash flow.

Mistake Three: Not Considering Fees

You will pay fees when you invest in mutual funds. And you don't want all of your profit to be eaten up by those fees. If you do, then what's the point of investing in the first place? Pay attention to fees before you spend money and make sure they are worth it.

Mistake Four: Forgetting All about Taxes

Taxes can take a big chunk out of your profits too and forgetting about them can leave you in a mess. Talk to your financial planner about taxes and make sure you understand how much you are going to end up paying to the government.

Mistake Five: Forgetting What You Are Trying to Do

You have a goal. Or at least you had a goal when you started this: become financially free.

If you forget that goal, you could end up wandering aimlessly in the world of mutual funds without ever actually accomplishing anything. You need to always keep your goals in mind and that will keep you on the right track.

Mutual funds sort of give you the best of both worlds between stocks and bonds. And they aren't locked in either if you want to sell. However, before deciding if they are right for you, be sure to look at the pros and cons. Nothing is ever perfect and that is something you have to consider before investing in mutual funds.

By working to avoid the mistakes and making smart decisions, then mutual funds could be the right way to go. Again, it all depends on your passion, what you want to do and what you want to avoid.

Before we can move on to other ways you can build your cash flow, we have one more market investment option to address: advanced markets. Then, we can get to another subject: Real Estate.

Chapter Ten

Types of Cash Flow Investments: Market Investments – Advanced Markets

I'm not going to lie to you. These advanced markets aren't easy to understand. They take a lot of work, research, and attention. They also require a great deal of brain power. You may not be interested in following this method, but there are advantages to options and futures, so they are worth checking into.

However, this is my disclosure: I am not going fully develop the discussion on advanced markets. There is simply just too much to cover. There is a reason why they are called "advanced." If you choose to take this path, you will need to conduct more research and likely consult a financial advisor before you spend any money. This is not something most can handle on their own. But I wanted to give you a brief overview so you know the opportunities exist.

Dynamic Investment Choices

There are a few different types of advanced markets we do need to cover. But like I said, I won't be going into extensive detail here. You will need a financial advisor for that, but let's get the basics.

Options Trading

Investopedia offers a definition of options:

> "An option is a contract that gives the buyer the right, but not the obligation, to buy or sell an underlying asset at a specific price on or before a certain date. An option, just like a stock or bond, is a security. It is also a binding contract with strictly defined terms and properties."

Options are aptly named because they give you choices. But that actually convolutes the issue even more – because you have to make good choices or you are going to lose money.

Okay, okay, okay… I know that none of this explains what options are in terms that you and I can actually grasp. Personally, I like examples. And you probably do too, so here's one that explains options a little better.

> *Let's say you want to buy a house and you don't want to go into debt. But, you won't have enough money to get it for three more months and that could mean you lose the house. You negotiate with the owner and they give you an option. You can buy the house in three months. However, while the original asking price was $175,000, in order to take this option, you will need to pay $178,000.*

Basically, you are paying extra to get the option. But, there are two different things that could happen at this point:

- The home turns out to be of serious historical significance and its value goes up to $400,000. Because you agreed to the option, the owner still has to sell it to you for $178,000. You will make a profit.

- The home is a money pit. The walls are full of asbestos and the pipes are all on the verge of busting. It's infested with rats and may/or may not be haunted. Suddenly, the house is worth nothing. Even though you agreed to an option, you can choose not to buy the house after all. The only thing you will be out is the $3,000.

That should make options clearer and easier to understand. They essentially give you an out. While you may lose some money, you won't lose all of it.

Two Types of Options

There are actually two different types of options you can choose:

- Call – This type allows the holder the chance to buy an asset at a price during a certain time frame. Effectively, you are hoping that the value will go up if the option expires.

- Put – With this type of option, you can choose to sell an option for a certain price. You are more or less hoping that the option will drop in value before it expires so you can sell out quicker.

Both types can work depending on the specific option you are buying.

The Pros and Cons of Options

When it comes to options, there is really only one pro and one con that you need to take into consideration. Remember that I am just skimming the surface here, so you will definitely want to talk more to a financial advisor before getting involved with options.

The Pro – You cannot lose more than the value of the option when you bought it. If you paid $200 for an option, then that's the very most you could lose. Remember that with stocks, it is actually possible to lose more than you spent.

The Con – You will actually have to pay for the option's time value. This means putting extra money into it. Additionally, if an option were to expire worthless, then you will lose everything you paid for it.

You don't really need to do much weighing of the pros and the cons before making a decision about options.

Common Beginner Mistakes with Options

Because options can be confusing and they are rather advanced, there are a few mistakes beginners are especially prone to make. You will absolutely want to avoid these mistakes so that you don't get tripped up before you even really get started.

Mistake One: Buying 'Out of the Money' Options

Many people turn to the 'out of the money' call options because they seem the safest. They don't come along with the same risks as other choices, but they aren't the best choice for most beginners.

That's because OTM calls, when you buy then outright, are extremely difficult ways to make money. In fact, they could result in regular money loss.

Mistake Two: Using an All-Purpose Strategy

When you get involved in options trading, you actually have a great deal of flexibility and leeway with what you can do. (Again, hire a financial planner to help you make the right choices). Using one investment strategy for everything just doesn't make sense.

When market conditions change, you have to be willing to go with the flow sometimes and use different strategies. Trying to do the same thing over and over again will not work and will likely result in losses.

Mistake Three: Not Having an Exit Plan

Because you are new to options, you may not even think of doing anything before the expiration date. But, waiting to the last minute could be very difficult. You need to actually create an exit plan before you get anywhere near the expiration date. That applies whether things are going your way or not. You don't know what could happen between the time you buy and the time the option expires. You need to be prepared to deal with any situation that comes up.

Mistake Four: Compromising Risk for Money

You need to know exactly how much you would like to risk. (Now keep in mind that "none at all" is never an option with investments). Then, you should always stay within your risk tolerance. Too many times, new investors will double the risk just to make up for one loss. The result could be detrimental.

Set your risk limits and stick with them.

Mistake Five: Choosing Illiquid Options

Liquidity is all about activity – or how fast you can buy or sell options. If something is illiquid, then you are stuck with it. It could remain inactive the whole time all the way up to the expiration date. That can leave you stuck and will certainly leave you twiddling your thumbs.

You will take a loss because you do usually pay the extra 10% for the option and that's money you will just lose when the asset is illiquid.

Mistake Six: Waiting too Long on Short Options

The whole purpose of short options is that, well, they are short! You shouldn't keep them very long and if you wait too long, you could lose money. Always be willing to buy back shorter options earlier than you expected for the best results.

If you work on avoiding these mistakes and issues, then options trading can be easier. But, keep in mind that they are never truly easy. I really do not recommend you jump into advanced markets all on your own or at all in the beginning. And, if you decide you are just dead set on them, then you absolutely have to have a financial planner. Otherwise, you will be jumping into the deep end when you don't even know how to swim.

Now, let's turn to futures.

Futures

The second type of advanced market investments you could choose is futures. Here's how Investopedia explains them:

> "A financial contract obligating the buyer to purchase an asset (or the seller to sell an asset), such as a physical commodity or a financial instrument, at a predetermined future date and price. Futures contracts detail the quality and quantity of the underlying asset; they are standardized to facilitate trading on a futures exchange."

Now, to make things easier, let's explain it this way:

> Futures are sort of like options except with one big difference. With options, you have the choice to buy or sell before the contract expires. If you buy futures, then you are obligated to stay in the contract until the expiration date.

Now, to make things a little clearer, I present you with a chart showing the comparison between options and futures.

As you can see, the main difference here is that you do have to follow some specific rules for futures. And the main one of these is that you are legally obligated to see the future to the end.

Issue	Futures	Options
Initial Margin or Deposit	Yes	No
Variation Margin	Yes	No
Speculation	Yes	Yes
Arbitrage	Yes	Yes
Barter Problems	No	No
Diversification	No	No
Liquid Market	Yes	Yes
Need for Speculators to Assume Risks	Yes	Yes
Hedge Any Currency	No	No
Legal Obligation	Yes	No

Being the Best Futures Trader Possible

You can never take the place of a financial planner unless you become one yourself, that is. But, what you can do is take steps to make yourself better – to be the best you possibly can.

Here are some actions you can take to make yourself better at futures trading.

Action One: Think Outside the Box

If you want to succeed at trading of any type, then you have to be willing to think on your own. You aren't a sheep. Don't act like one. Learn how to follow your own path to profit and "The New Retirement."

The same thing doesn't work for everyone and even in futures trading, there is no one cookie cutter answer. Think outside the box. Be independent. Make decisions based on your own research. That's when you will be able to make the best decisions.

Action Two: Analyze Everything

You have to develop analysis skills. If you don't already have them, then this is something to work on. The more you can analyze both technical and fundamental matters in futures, the better off you will be.

Even in your leisure time, read books and magazines on the subject. Go to future released websites and learn more. Practice futures trading on paper. Do everything you can to be constantly learning and finding new methods of both analysis and practice.

Action Three: Learn All the Time

You have to be an active learner. In fact, since none of us knows everything (including me) you always have to research and take the chance to learn something new. You can go to seminars and events, read online, read books, and do everything you can to find out about futures trading.

Never stop learning. That means keep learning tomorrow, next month, next year, and twenty years in the future.

Action Four: Always Get Information

There are plenty of tools of the trade that you can use to keep practicing and to make smart decisions with futures. Use the Internet to get real time stock quotes. Look for software that will let you analyze the markets and make trades. Look for tools that will help you make smart decisions quickly and decisively.

Four Mistakes That Can Mess Up Futures

I don't know how to tell you enough. Futures and options too are very advanced and they can be very difficult, especially for a beginner. If you choose to go this route, then you absolutely need a financial planner. You also need to know the mistakes to avoid. So, here are four mistakes that people could make with futures. Avoid them and you will have that going for you!

Mistake One: Not Following a System

Let's say you get started with futures and things seem to be actually going quite well. Suddenly, you think, "I could just change this or that" because you want to do better and better. But, you know the saying "leave well enough alone." If something is working, why would you change it?

Doing that could take a big risk with your money and it may not turn out the way you wanted. So, if you have a system and it is working well, don't mess with it.

Mistake Two: Not Worrying about Risk

When you invest, there is always risk. That's just reality.

But that doesn't mean you should ignore risk and just run around willy-nilly doing whatever strikes your fancy. That' a great way to lose your money especially when dealing with advanced markets like futures.

Work on limiting your losses to levels you are comfortable with. Learn how to buy 'stops' to avoid raising your losses too high. Find out how buying 'puts' can minimize loss as well. The more you can do to protect your money, the better.

Mistake Three: Not Staying Focused

It is easy to get distracted when it comes to trading any type of stocks. However, when it comes to futures, you have to pay attention all of the time. It's not something you can look at every once in a while.

If you hire a financial planner, then some of this will be off your plate so that you can deal with other responsibilities. Just make sure you are always aware of what is going on and always keep your goals in mind so as not to stray from your purpose of financial freedom.

Mistake Four: Not Considering New Ideas

While it is a good idea to stick with a method that works, this doesn't mean you can't be open to new ideas. You may think you are a great trader and you are making all the right choices. That doesn't mean, though, that there's not something else you could learn.

Always be researching and keep moving forward. When you have a chance to learn, take it, and always be open to new ideas.

If you avoid these mistakes, then handling futures will be easier. But, don't get too big for your britches and think this means you know enough to handle it on your own. You still need a financial planner.

Cannot Be Taken Lightly

Now, there's a lot more to these advanced markets. Otherwise, they wouldn't them called advanced in the first place. They cannot be taken lightly and they are not something you can buy and sell on a whim. Before you even consider getting involved in advanced markets, you will need to learn a great deal more about them. This is truly only tapping the surface.

And, you should never invest your money into anything until you know everything possible about it. Only then can you be certain of your decisions.

You Will Need to Do Your Research

Your final thought to remember when it comes to advanced markets is to always do your research. That should include learning things on your own and consulting a financial planner. However, keep in mind that you need to know what you are doing without just letting the planner do everything for you.

Don't be a sheep!

It is your money, so know exactly where it is going instead of expecting someone else to keep up with everything for you.

For your research, here are some helpful resources (websites and books):

- www.nasdaq.com/investing
- www.Investopedia.com
- www.MoneyChimp.com
- www.WallStreetSurvivor.com
- *The Little Book of Common Sense Investing*
- *Stock Investing for Dummies*
- *Stock Market for Beginners*
- *The Five Rules for Successful Stock Investing*

Those resources should help you extensively, whether you want to go to the online sources or you want to read books. Just make sure you can find out as much as possible. Then, hire a financial planner.

How to Choose a Financial Planner

Okay, so I have told you over and over again that you need a financial planner. And, believe me, that is good advice. But how exactly do you choose a financial planner? Through research, of course.

Here is a checklist you can use to make the right decision.

- Look at their qualifications. You need to know what titles they have, what certifications they have, and what makes them qualified to do the work.

- Check the advisor's form ADV with the US Securities and Exchange Commission. It should be clean. If it isn't, then don't hire that manager.

- Find out what securities licenses they hold.

- Look at their quarterly report to see how they have done with other peoples' money.

- Find out their fees and payments. You need to know if they are going to get paid even if they lose your money, etc.

- Always read the contract and the fine print carefully. You need to know what you are getting into.

- Make sure you can communicate well with the advisor and you feel they communicate well with you.

If you look for these things, then you should be able to hire an advisor that you can depend on to do right by your money.

And, let's face it, the last thing you would want to happen is someone to run off with all your cash!

Now, before we move on to a different investment option altogether, here are some final points on market investments.

- Not all stocks will work as cash flow for you. You need to research any stock before you decide to buy.

- Stocks, bonds, mutual funds, and advanced markets all include different levels of risk, so you do need to do your research.

- Don't just buy a bond. You need to understand all of the terms associated with the bond before you spend any money on it.

- Mutual funds have different pay out structures. They may pay monthly, quarterly, semi-annually, or annually. You need to know how this may affect your cash flow.

Before you get involved in market investing, you have to know what you are doing. This isn't something you can just jump into on your own. You need to do two things: research and consult a financial advisor.

Now that we have talked about all of your different market investment options, it's time to move on to another topic – one of my favorites too – Real Estate.

Chapter Eleven:

Real Estate

Now we are to my favorite topic and my favorite method of investing for an early and quite comfortable retirement. We are going to talk about Real Estate. There are so many reasons why I choose Real Estate over any other investment option and I am happy to share them with you. We are going to spend some time talking about everything Real Estate has to offer and then you can decide for yourself if this will be your favorite investment option or not.

The Success of Real Estate Investing

I want to give you a little insight into what Real Estate investing has done for other people. I feel like I should put a disclaimer on here though: something like 'results not typical'. I can't guarantee you are going to become a billionaire through Real Estate investing. But I can guarantee that, if you want to, you can find it a successful endeavor. Here's proof: Forbes created a list of billionaires and 20 of them are Real Estate investors (or tycoons if you will):

- Lee Shau Kee, worth $19.6 billion.
- Cheng Yu-Tung, worth $16.2 billion.
- Wang Jianlin, worth $15.1 billion.
- Donald Bren, worth $14.4 billion.
- Gerald Cavendish Grosvenor, worth $13 billion.
- Thomas and Raymond Kwok, worth $12.6 billion.
- David and Simon Reuben, worth $11.5 billion.
- Robert and Phillip Ng, worth $11 billion.
- Joseph Lau, worth $8.4 billion.
- Peter Woo, worth $7.2 billion.
- Yang Huiyan, worth $6.9 billion.
- Charles Cadogan, worth $6.9 billion.
- Robert Lefrak, worth $6.1 billion.
- Chan Laiwa, worth $6 billion.
- Hui Ka Yan, worth $5.7 billion.
- Hui Wing Mau, worth $5.7 billion.
- Stephen Ross, worth $5.4 billion.
- Kwee, worth $5.2 billion.
- Harry Triguboff, worth $5 billion.
- Walter Kwok, worth $5 billion.

And, that is just the list of top billionaires who have made their money through Real Estate investing. There's no way to list here the countless people who have become millionaires through this method – or those who have a comfortable life but aren't quite millionaires.

In all of history, this has been the most successful investment option out there and it gets proven time and time again.

So, here's your chance. Do you want to jump on the Real Estate investment train or not? Again, you may not become a billionaire like one of those people I named above, but you can be successful.

Let's talk a bit about why.

A Tangible Asset

Real Estate is the only truly tangible asset. You aren't buying a piece of paper that owns a part of a company. You are actually buying property – land, buildings, homes, etc. You are purchasing something and it can offer big returns.

> *"Yeah, yeah, yeah," you think.*

> *"I have heard it all" you say.*

You believe you might just know everything there is to know about what Real Estate has to offer and the bad sides too. Well, maybe you know SOME things – maybe even a lot – but you don't know everything. I mean come on, if you knew it all then you would already be a retired Millennial and you wouldn't be reading this book.

But, you are reading this book, so you recognize that you still have things to learn.

Forget for a moment what you may already know about Real Estate and let's talk about all the reasons why so many people choose this option.

You Are in Control

It gives you options. The control over it is one reason why people really like Real Estate. You could pick from land, homes, multifamily property, commercial properties, hotels, office buildings, retail space, etc. It is up to you and you can choose what you like (after research, of course!).

On a side note here: land is not usually a good cash flow investment. It doesn't really do anything but sit there. So when you are trying to build cash flow, you will want to avoid this one.

Appreciation

Properties tend to appreciate. We will talk about depreciation in a bit. But, keep in mind that if you invest in Real Estate in a growing area, it will go up in value and that means you can bring in a hefty profit.

Long-Term Options

Real Estate offers a long-term investment. You could choose to buy a property and continue profiting from it for years. Eventually, you may choose to sell, but you don't have to and you can still profit from it.

A Great Hedge

Real Estate is often considered a hedge against the dangers of the stock market and other risky investments. It also will hedge against inflation (you know how things keep costing more and the dollar keeps getting more and more worthless). No matter what happens with money, Real Estate will always be valuable.

The Power of Leverage

Real Estate investing is also a fantastic way of leveraging. In other words, when you invest, you are actually enhancing your earning potential. Most people consider Real Estate the easiest way to leverage your money efficiently.

Tax Relief

If you know much about taxes, then you know that Real Estate investments can really help you here. There are lots of different things you can claim on taxes including:

- Maintenance and Repairs
- Interest Paid
- Property Taxes and Rates
- Insurance Payments
- Agent Fees
- Travel to and From the Property
- Interest on the Mortgage (if there is one)
- Depreciation of the Building

In other words, you can save a lot of money when it is tax time. And who doesn't want to do that? Come on! Almost all of us dread April 15. And this can take some of that dread away.

Expect Reliable Returns

Stocks may give you the chance to get really big returns. However, there is also a risk that you could lose everything. The problem is that stocks aren't fully reliable. When you invest in Real Estate, you will get a great deal more of that reliability you are looking for. The market may change, but it takes much more time for it to do so.

And when you invest in rental property, you will (usually) get reliable payments every month – as long as the tenants do what they say they will. So, there is much more reliability to this. You don't have to feel like you are taking as much of a risk.

In other words, this very tangible asset has a lot to offer, making Real Estate a fantastic investment option.

Passive or Aggressive

When you choose to invest in Real Estate, you get the option be as passive or as aggressive as you would like. That goes for what you buy and when, how you manage your property, etc.

For example:

> Let's say you buy a multifamily dwelling, like a small apartment building that has five or six apartments. You can be in-control, managing the whole thing on your own, dealing with issues as they arise, choosing tenants, fixing broken things, and so on.

> Or

> You can hire a property manager. This person will actually act as the go-between. You can make all the big decisions, but everything else will be handled for you.

Real Estate investing really gives you a lot of freedom to handle things the way that you would like.

Higher Cost of Ownership but Great Extras

The one thing that scares people the most about real estate investing is the high cost of investment. You can buy stocks and bonds for a few thousand dollars or less. You can't exactly buy a house for that price. There's a lot of expense that goes into it:

- The cost to purchase a property (and you don't want to go into debt again so you need cash)
- Maintenance and repair costs
- Costs that accrue if a rental property stands vacant
- Property taxes
- Property management costs if you hire one

It all adds up and those numbers can get scary. But you do have to look at the big picture here – the forest and not just the trees. There are plenty of "extras" you get that come just from owning property.

Of course, we talked a little about tax advantages, but let's give them some more attention. Here are the top ten tax advantages you will gain. And they are just the beginning.

1. You get to claim depreciation. Yes, you read that right. Even though your Real Estate is probably appreciating, it is perfectly legal to claim depreciation on any property you own every year for up to 27.5 years.

2. You get to depreciate the things that make your property livable too. That includes anything that will wear out over time, including hot water heaters, the air conditioner and heater, plumbing, electrical fixtures, etc.

3. If you have an investment property, you get a deduction or insurance, utilities, and Real Estate taxes.

4. Any repairs you need to make to ensure a property is livable or any supplies you need to buy can also be written off.

5. If you hire a management company for your Real Estate, you have to pay commissions and fees, but you can write them off too.

6. If you actually live in the Real Estate you have purchased and you work from home, then you can write off your home office. This includes a portion of all home expenses such as taxes, insurance, utilities, phones, etc.

7. With the home office, any office supplies and equipment you need counts too, including cell phones, computers, printers, envelopes, stamps, paper, pens, staplers, etc. Essentially, if you have to buy something related to your investments business, then you can deduct it.

8. When you have business expenses related to your Real Estate investing, then you have another deduction. This could include subscriptions to professional publications, travel to events, travel to the property to make repairs, membership into professional Real Estate investment groups, advertisements, dues, and using the Internet for the company to search for Real Estate opportunities.

9. If you have to use your personal vehicle to drive to properties for repairs, for purchase, or for anything else, then you can deduct mileage on your taxes too.

10. And if you want even more tax deductions, you can get them by becoming a qualified Real Estate professional. You would be surprised at how much you will be able to deduct in this way.

Don't let the high cost of investing in Real Estate scare you away. There are actually numerous advantages that you will be able to enjoy, especially when tax time comes around.

Breaking the Myths

Now, I know that a lot of you will go out and do research online. That's a good thing. You should. But, you also have to be careful of what you believe and what you do not. There are plenty of myths floating around online that are easy to believe if you are a beginner to this world. Let's go ahead and dispel those myths right now.

Myth One: A Recovering Housing Market Means No Room for Investors

The housing market goes up and down and then up and down again, even worse than Jack and Jill fetching their pail of water. And if you talk to the wrong people, they will tell you that investing in Real Estate when the housing market has gone down or is recovering is a mistake.

And, yes, there is a risk to investing in Real Estate, especially when the housing market is struggling. However, that risk can be calculated. As long as you do your research and act carefully, then you can minimize that risk and still reap great reward.

Another thing you have to remember is that because the housing market has struggled for so long, people just stopped building houses. That means even though there are more people wanting to buy, there isn't as much Real Estate available. Meaning, if you invest, you do have the potential to bring in more income if you choose to sell. And the shortage also means you will be able to charge more in rent.

Myth Two: Past Performance of Investments Provide a Good Predictor

What goes around comes around.

You have to learn from the past.

If you don't learn from your mistakes, then you are doomed to repeat it.

These are the kinds of things we hear often about the past. And people will likely tell you that if you look at the tenuous past of the Real Estate market, you may be convinced that this is not the way to go.

While the past can be somewhat of a predictor of the future, you have to learn from the successes and failures equally.

Of course, you should never make reckless decisions and you should never make your choices on speculation. Make the decisions carefully and no matter what happened in the past, you will still be able to find success.

Myth Three: Investing in Real Estate Means Investing in Money Pits

Well, this can depend. If you buy a total money pit because you didn't do your research, then that is what you can expect. However, if you make your investment decisions wisely, then it won't be such a problem.

Keep in mind that a Real Estate investment is an investment. You are going to have to put some money into it. You may have to make some repairs or replace some things. That doesn't mean you have invested in a pit.

Then, there is the concern that investing in Real Estate means spending all of your time dealing with it. That's up to you too. Chris Clothier explains:

> *"The idea that real estate investment is a huge time sink, though, is largely due to the idea that investors have to act as landlords to their properties. While some choose to do so, it's not necessary. Investors can hire property management companies, or better yet look to turnkey investing to keep things manageable. It simply takes organization, and*

smart investors can leverage good people to prevent them from getting buried in a time sink."

How much money you spend on investments and how much time you deal with it all depends on your own choices.

Myth Four: You Can Only Invest Locally

Some people will tell you that you should only invest in properties that are local to you. And, yes, there are some advantages to that. You will know more about the market, the economy, the neighborhoods, the people, and more. But that doesn't mean you absolutely have to stay local.

You can branch out to other markets and that will give you many more opportunities. All this means, though, is that you will have to be more careful with your research. It's not a good idea to just walk into an unknown market and buy something. You need to pay attention to what you are doing.

Myth Five: You Have to Avoid Risks in Investing

Some people are so afraid of risk that they don't ever take any chances. The problem is that without risk, there is no reward. You cannot make money from investments without taking a few chances.

In fact, I would recommend that you embrace risk. Go out there and take a chance to ensure you have the best opportunity for profits.

But there is a difference between calculated risks and risks for the sake of making them. As long as you do your research and take the time to look at your options carefully, then you can enjoy all of the rewards.

Mistakes in Real Estate Investing

Here's the thing about real estate investing: it can cost you big money if you make a mistake. You have spent so much time getting out of debt. Why would you put yourself right back into it because something you did bombed? The best way to avoid a big problem is to avoid mistakes.

You can learn from those people who have made these mistakes before you. While it didn't help them much, it can definitely help you.

Mistake One: Winging It

When it comes to Real Estate, or any other investment option for that matter, you just can't wing it. You can wing it when it comes to lunch, but when you are investing in something, you need to plan for it.

The best way to come up with a plan is to decide your goal and then work backwards to determine what steps you need to take.

The worst time you could come up with a strategy would be after you have made a purchase. That's too late. That would be like trying to decide where you want to eat lunch after you have sat down in a restaurant.

Create a plan in advance and it will help you make smart choices.

Mistake Two: Thinking It Is a Get Rich Quick Scheme

Like I said, Real Estate is my favorite investment choice for people working toward "The New Retirement." It can and will succeed. It will not, however, make you rich in one day. Just like everything else, it will take work and time. And it will take your attention.

If you put time into it, then this can be very successful. If you think you are going to flip a property and wake up rich, you will be sorely disappointed.

Mistake Three: Trying to Do It All on Your Own

You can't do anything on your own. Trying to is not going to go so well. I promise. It won't work. Don't try it.

When it comes to Real Estate, there are numerous times when you need other people to help you out. If you are repairing a property so that you can sell it, then there is no sense risking electrocution to wire something yourself. Instead, hire contractors to handle the really serious work.

If you are renting your property out, then you could hire property managers to handle little day to day issues so that you can be less hands on.

Mistake Four: Overpaying

Here's one of the most problematic issues that investors run into. They are so eager to get a property that they overpay and soon realize there is no room left for a profit. That's not a chance you can take when you want to become a retired Millennial. Take the time to do research. Look into buying lesser valued properties such as foreclosures. And be very careful to avoid overpaying so that you do still have room to make money.

Mistake Five: Not Doing Your Homework

I know, you aren't in school anymore. You are done with homework, right? No! Homework is extremely important whenever you are investing money. You can always learn something new about Real Estate investing so take the time to study. Go to Real Estate investors meetings. Do everything you can to learn more and more.

Mistake Six: Not Paying Attention to Cash Flow

Your goal should always be to build cash flow no matter what you invest in. I know I keep bringing it up, but it is that important – and a key point in this book! When you invest in Real Estate, it is easy to lose track of cash flow and ond up property poor.

Before you get started with any project, take the time to set up your budget, account for expenses, and ensure you are maintaining cash flow.

Mistake Seven: Getting Yourself Stuck

Do you want to paint yourself into a corner? Do you want to have to stand there while the paint dries or crawl on the counter to avoid stepping on it? If you paint yourself into a corner with Real Estate investing, you could find yourself with a property you can't get off your hands. That costs a lot of money.

Always look for properties you can purchase at below market value and then sell for a profit or rent out for steady income. Whatever you do, always have an exit strategy for your project.

Mistake Eight: Not Calculating Estimates Right

If you are planning on rehabbing a property, then there will be estimates involved for all of the repairs. If you don't know what you are doing, there is a very good chance you will underestimate your costs and end up blowing your budget.

If you don't know how to accurately estimate costs, then do homework and learn from the experts. Then, create real, well thought out estimates that will keep you as close to budget as possible.

Real Estate can be an exciting and fun way to build your cash flow, bit if you make mistakes, it won't work. Make sure you avoid these issues for the best results right from your first Real Estate purchase.

The Bottom Line of Real Estate Ownership

I went over a lot, I know. I get really excited when I start talking about Real Estate. However, I wanted to sum everything up for you one more time. Here's the bottom line when it comes to Real Estate:

- You get multiple tax advantages and they come to you on a federal, state, and local level.

- This can be a very passive investment if you choose a property manager. However, you can choose for it to be less passive if you would like.

- You can use leverage to purchase real estate property.

That's the main thing you need to glean from this as far as choosing Real Estate as your method of bringing in cash flow.

Now, I want to talk about one more method of investing that is special to our generation specifically. We Millennials have an advantage in knowing so much technology and having it at our fingertips. So, we will discuss eCommerce and other online opportunities next.

Chapter Twelve:

Online/eCommerce

Thanks to the leaps and bounds in technology we have enjoyed over the last few years, there are plenty of business opportunities just waiting for you. You probably know a bit about this area, but there is still plenty to learn. I will overview the main areas, which may or may not be review for you, but open the doors to ideas – and, yes, a need for further research. While Real Estate may be my favorite investment vehicle, that doesn't mean I don't love eCommerce and online opportunities as well.

It is time to embark on the technology world and get started looking at the opportunities you have at your fingertips. There may be more options than you could possibly realize and I am certain this chapter will not cover them all.

In fact, there are almost an infinite number of online business types you could choose from. We only have space enough to talk about a few of those – but it should be enough to get you started in your path to financial freedom with "The New Retirement".

Best Area of Concentration

Let's talk about us for a minute – you and me and every other Millennial out there. We have something going for us. We are possibly the most technologically gifted generation to date (but watch out for Generation Z. They are coming and they may know more than us so we do have to keep up).

For many of us, getting started online is quick and easy because we already know the online world – for the most part. We don't have the learning curve that other generations may have to face, so getting started online doesn't take much work, time, or effort. We can dive right in, feet first, and not worry about sinking.

The beauty of the online job (in addition to it not costing much to get it going) is that there is something you can do no matter what your passion. Everyone has something they enjoy and all you have to do is look for the right option online.

I want to make one thing clear. While Real Estate may be my favorite, I believe that online and eCommerce options are actually the best for us Millennials, especially as you get started on pursuing your passion and living "The New Retirement."

Why I am so strong on it?

Well, to begin with, most Millennials don't exactly have much money. I mean come on – I know people my age who are still living on Ramen noodles, a la college days. Real Estate and market investments cost some significant money to even get started. They may not be an option in the beginning – but later, they can definitely enhance what you will have already gained by working, and earning, within the virtual world.

Most importantly, Millennials have the techie advantage. We know how to work the Internet and we handle it well. Why wouldn't we want to start with an arena we already have some comfort in? Some of it can even seem like child's play to us. It only makes sense.

Finally, there is literally a bajillion (okay, maybe not that many, but you get what I mean) different niches and topics out there on the Internet, it is easy for any of us to find something to do. So just begin right now (well after a bit of research to set your sights in clear focus).

> Log on to Facebook.
> Create a website.
> Start affiliate marketing.
> Write a blog.
> Write an eBook.

Just do something and you will be surprised at how much the Internet has to offer.

Online Marketing Myths

Here's the thing I love about the Internet – it offers a limitless source of information and it makes it easy for anyone to do business with anyone in the world.

Here's the thing I hate about the Internet – not all the information is reliable and it is a great way to spread myths.

Before you believe everything you read, let's bust some myths that have been floating around about online marketing.

Myth One: Any Clicks Will Increase Sales

If you want clicks, you can get them. You can get a ton of traffic to your website by using generic keywords. But just because you got a thousand clicks doesn't mean you will get a single sale.

You need quality clicks and that means driving the right kind of traffic to your website. The wrong kind will be useless.

What do I mean?

Let's say you sell web design services specifically and no other graphics design. If your keyword is just design, then you could get people looking for graphics, logo, interior, and a plethora of other design searches. They may click, but they won't do business with you. You would need to ensure that your key words say web design services.

Myth Two: It Worked for Them...It Will Work for You

If everything in life had cookie cutter answers, imagine how simple everything would be? We could just do what someone else did and be all the better for it. Hear the snap if my fingers and wake up, buttercup! It doesn't work that way and we all know it.

What worked for one company when it comes to online marketing probably won't work the same way for you. No, you don't have to reinvent the wheel, but you do need to remember that you should tailor any marketing plan to your business and your goals for it to work properly. It may be similar, but needs to represent you and your needs.

Myth Three: Blog the Hell Out of What Your Company Is Doing

OMG our company just pained the walls!
Look at this new plant we got!
We sell the best products everrrr!

Do you think that's what works? Of course not! I'll go into in more detail in the blogging section, but remember this: blog about things readers will actually care about. That is how you get them to read your content – and just maybe pay you for your services.

Myth Four: It's Impossible to Get Found on the Internet

A lot of people worry that since there are millions of websites out there, it is impossible for one little one to get found. That's the beauty of search engine marketing and optimization. Essentially, it's up to you whether or not you get found. When you do the right things, you can move up to the first page of Google. And that, my friend, will almost guarantee you to be found.

Myth Five: You Have to Be on Every Social Media Platform Possible

Yes, you do need an online presence on many social media platforms. No, you don't have to be on every single one all of the time. Here are the ones I consider essential:

- Facebook
- Twitter
- Google+
- LinkedIn

And, here are the ones you could use depending on the nature of your business:

- Instagram
- Pinterest
- Tumblr
- Snapchat
- Vine
- YouTube

Start with the basics and as you expand you can add more. But some social media platforms just don't matter for businesses.

Myth Six: Company Emails Always Get Deleted

Emails are what you make of them. If you send spam, then it will get treated like spam and deleted (and it will look really bad for your business too).

If you send quality information that gives readers a reason to open that email, you would be surprised at how many do.

Myth Seven: A Perfect Website Will Get Attention

There's actually a little truth to this. You do need an aesthetically pleasing website. If you build crap that looks like it belongs on AngelFire from back in the day and you have a curser that has glitter following it around, you will turn people off in a heartbeat.

So, yes, you need a killer website. But, no, it will not get attention all on its own. You have to promote your website. You need to share it on social media. Include it on marketing materials. Make sure you have your SEO in order. That's the kind of stuff that will see results.

Myth Eight: Online Marketing Is a Waste

Well, again, there could be some truth to this. If you make mistakes and you believe all of those myths we already discussed, then it could be a waste. You may put a lot of time and effort into it and not see anything in return. That does happen.

But when used correctly and consistently, then online marketing can be powerful.

Now, get past those myths.

Accept the truth and learn how to use online marketing for all the power it offers…in other words, "use the force, Luke." (If that reference was too old or obscure, I am hearkening back to classic *Star Wars*. It's an oldie, but goodie.)

Now, let's get back to the specifics of how you can harness the power of the Internet for your future life of financial freedom.

Did you know that you can make money on Facebook? On Twitter? Other social media sites?

As a Millennial, you are most likely aware of this, but I will review as refresher! And for those for whom this is new material, I will start with this: The "Big Idea" sites are what I call the steamrollers – those websites that pretty much tell the world "get out of my way or get crushed." You can probably start ticking them off on your hand right now. While there are many other social media sites to be aware of, I am going to focus on these four:

- Facebook
- Google
- LinkedIn
- Twitter

These types of sites actually have opportunities you may not have even known existed, so let's look at each of them a little closer.

Facebook

> *Click the like button.*
> *Follow me.*
> *Look at this page.*
> *Share.*

Facebook could arguably be called the biggest and baddest of the all of the websites on the Internet. It has millions of users who are active every day. It only makes sense that it will play an absolute vital role in your goals for making money online (yes, you should set clear goals as we discussed back in chapter two).

Here's how:

- Create a badass Facebook page for whatever online business you choose. A lot of people will find you on the social network before they would have ever even though to look for your website.

- Post often and publicly. Make sure your friends on your personal Facebook page know about your business and then continually post on the business page and interact with followers regularly.

- Build and push ads. Facebook has a pretty cool advertising program. You can sponsor a post you made on a business page so it keeps coming up in people's newsfeeds. You can create an ad that shows up over to the right side of the screen too. The best part is you can fully target everything. You choose who sees your ads so you don't waste money on the wrong demographic.

Facebook is great for building an online business because it gives people another chance to find you. It also gives you the chance to interact with your followers. And the more you do that, the more trusted of a name you will become.

It may seem like a lot of effort, but believe me, it's worth it.

Google

Google has a nifty little thing called AdSense and it can give you a great opportunity to make more money. When you create an AdSense account, a magical thing can happen – well maybe it is not magical since Google seems capable of doing anything they want – but still, it is pretty cool.

Google can match ads to search results. Then, when people search for certain keywords, they will see your ad first as sort of a sponsored listing. And if you know people at all, you also know that most of them are more likely to click on the very first search result than anything else.

If you have a website, then this is considered one of the top preferred methods of driving traffic to your site and thus your company.

LinkedIn

Don't ignore LinkedIn.

Don't think it is blah or boring either. This is a website that you need to use.

LinkedIn is the business person's Facebook. But, a lot of people make a mistake. They create their little LinkedIn professional profile and then they don't do anything else. But it's not a static thing. You can actually use it to make money.

Dave Kerpen points out the following:

> *"16 million.*
>
> *That's how many people viewed my blog content on LinkedIn last year. Those 16 million page views led to 300,000 followers, thousands of sales leads and books sold and more than $1 million of revenue."*

That's how well one blogger did on LinkedIn. Just one. Now, that may not happen for everyone, but it doesn't mean LinkedIn shouldn't be in your scope of attention.

All you have to do is create a killer profile with an awesome photo, perfect headline, and concise information. Then, you can start creating blog posts and share them on all of your social media. These blogs should start getting attention and when they do, this will turn into leads and sales and followers.

Twitter

Then, there is Twitter. You can only write a post of 140 words or less, so there is surely no way you could make money, right? Of course there is! In fact, there are many ways. Here are just a few:

1. Turn followers into your cheerleaders – when they re-tweet your tweets, this gets more attention.

2. Actually advertise and sell products through Tweets.

3. Gain leads through quality Tweets.

4. Use Twitter to find followers and therefore customers from around the world.

Since Twitter is short and sweet, it is an easy way to get to people without losing their attention.

Big idea sites have a lot to offer because they are so, well, big. And, they make a fantastic method for boosting an online business that you already have in another shape or form.

Social Media Marketing Mistakes to Avoid

Social media marketing is relatively new for many people. But as a tech savvy Millennial, it shouldn't be an issue for you. After all, we Millennials have virtually cut our teeth on technology. That still doesn't mean you know everything and it always helps to know what mistakes to avoid.

Mistake One: Having No Strategy

> *"I'm going to just jump on Facebook and create an ad."*

> *"Maybe I should post something on Twitter today."*

> *"Oh, I guess I could Instagram that."*

None of that works – not for a business that is. And since you are building an online business, you can't just sporadically hop on and do something. You have to be consistent and you need a strategy. The great thing is you can create a strategy however you want:

- Decide how many followers you want to get in the next month.
- Set a goal at how many clicks to your website you want to achieve.
- Choose your plan for posts on a social media a certain number of times each week.
- Create an advertising campaign and use it across all of your social media sites.

Whatever you do, you need to have a reason behind it and a method you are going to employ to accomplish it.

Mistake Two: Getting in Over Your Head

There are a lot of social media options out there and I would venture to guess you have accounts on more than one or two of them. That's fine. But when you are working on this new business venture, you don't want to get in over your head too quickly. If you do, problems will arise. Why?

When it comes to promoting a business on social media, you have to baby it. You have to pay attention to it every day no matter what else you have going on. If you ignore or neglect it, you could lose out on followers and you could make your brand fall back.

Don't get in over your head too quickly. Start with a couple of sites like Facebook and Twitter. Then, add in LinkedIn, Instagram, YouTube, and Pinterest as needed. That will let you get used to working with one before you add another.

Mistake Three: Paying for Followers

Have you ever heard of *black hat*? Black hat refers to shady and sometimes illegal methods of getting things done on the Internet (there was even a movie about it). Often, people turn to black hat methods to spam email accounts, hide text in websites, etc. Paying for fake followers is one of these methods.

For one thing, it doesn't do anything for your business and it will not increase ROI (Return on Investment). It may seem to look good if you have more followers, but it won't accomplish anything. Fake accounts are shady and often get deleted, leaving you with a follower drop pretty quickly too.

Mistake Four: Selling Constantly

So, you have put together your Facebook page and you are ready to put your business out there. You have two options:

1. Make every single post about selling your product or brand. Make them pushy. Post often.
2. Provide real, interesting information that will engage followers. Interact when you can. Post on a consistent basis.

Which do you think will work better? If you ever have been to a car dealership, then you know the answer. You know what it's like to walk on a car lot and have a salesmen breathing down your neck literally trying to push you into buying something. It's uncomfortable and people don't like it.

Don't be the virtual car salesperson. While some content should be geared toward sales, you also need to provide information that is interesting, funny, emotional, unique, or engaging in some other way. That's the way to get people interested in your business.

Mistake Five: Going Overboard With Hashtags

As you know, most social media sites use hashtags these days to make it easy for people to find things. Twitter, Instagram, and Facebook all use them and they are very important for anything you post. But let's face it, you can go overboard with them. If you just go nuts and hashtag all over the place, you look unprofessional.

For the sake of an example, you post a picture of the sunset over the Rocky Mountains in Colorado (because you are based in Colorado and sell something really cool made locally). Your hashtags could look something like this:

> *#sunset #Colorado #ColorfulColorado #RockyMountains #Rockies #YourBusinessName #YourCityName #BeautifulColors #PictureoftheDay*

Or like this:

> *#sunset #Colorado #Colorful #Colorado #Rocky #Mountains #Rockies #YourBusinessName #YourCityName #Beautiful #Colors #GoRockies #WeMissTulo #HikingtheMountains #ColoradoBeer #PartyNight #DrinkingBuddies #AvalancheRules #Native #ColoradoNative #GoHomeNonNatives #TakingPictures #PrettyPictures #WhatYouDoing #PhotographerinTraining #GettingHigh #MileHighCity*

I can't even begin to describe the problems with the second example. Anything associated with your business probably shouldn't talk about drinking beer, getting high, and partying unless you just happen to own a liquor store, a marijuana dispensary, or a party planning service. But most importantly, it is just too many hashtags and most of them have nothing to do with anything.

Use hashtags, but only when they apply to your business or the picture in some way. Go overboard and you will end up looking like a teenage girl who posts selfies and tags them like crazy.

The bottom line is it is just downright annoying. Don't be annoying – annoying loses customers and money.

Mistake Six: Not Proofreading

Your posts have to look good and you have to look professional. Grammatical errors will hurt your credibility. And no I don't care if it was net-speak. It doesn't belong in a professional post. You have to proofread.

Want an example? Which of the following two looks better?

> *Where are u wen you need a cellphone cover? Don't drop your phone in the water and hope itz wrking. Buy our cellphone covers.*

> OR

> *Where are you when you need a cellphone cover? Don't drop your phone in water and hope it keeps working. Protect it today and buy our new cellphone covers.*

Obviously, there is a clear winner here because it is all about grammar and proofreading.

Mistake Seven: Forgetting that Social Media Is Social

The final mistake is one that people make often just because they are busy and they forget the whole purpose of social media in the first place. They post something and then never look at it again.

Social media is called "social" for a reason. It is all about interacting. And you will build more loyal followers when you remember this.

- If people comment on your posts, reply to them!
- If they post to your page, like it and reply.
- If they have a complaint, contact them via private messenger.

Always be social and interact. Ask them questions and then respond when they give answers. Answer their questions. Thank them for compliments. Thank them for complaints even. Show you are engaged. Social media should always be social.

Social media and the "Big Idea" sites can be super powerful as long as you avoid those mistakes.

Niche Affiliate Sites

One of the great things about the Internet is that you don't have to do everything and sell everything. In fact, you can be much more successful if you work within a niche. And the super fantastic thing is that there are literally millions of different niches out there. The truth is, you can be pretty damn specific with your product or service and still have plenty of an audience since virtually everyone can get online and find you.

And here is the beauty of affiliate marketing: you don't even have to have a product. Essentially, you are selling something for someone else and making money from it.

Of course, making a profit from niche affiliate sites means knowing how to build something that will actually work. After all, we all know that "if you build an amazing niche affiliate site, then they will come and buy things." Okay, that isn't exactly the quote from the Kevin Costner movie, but you get the gist.

Here are some ways you can create a niche affiliate website that does work:

- You can create a product review site. Essentially, you get paid to write product reviews by the sellers of those products. Then, you post those reviews on your website. That's all you have to do. However, you need to create honest reviews. If you are always positive and you always act like every product is perfect, no one will believe you and your site will not be effective.

- Blogging is invaluable when it comes to affiliate sites. People will pay you to blog, but what you write has to actually be good. Either make sure you have the capability of writing good, readable material or consider hiring a freelance writer to come up with the information.

- Create a price comparison site. People like these sites because they provide real, practical information. They can easily comparison shop all at one place without having to go visit the websites or physical stores for every seller.

- Look to coupon and discount sites. These sites are appealing to the public too because they give access to lower prices. Businesses will pay niche affiliate sites to feature coupons and discounts because this will drive more traffic to them.

- Get unusual. The great thing about niche marketing is that you can fit into whatever niche you want. In fact, the more unusual the better. That's because you likely won't have as much competition.

  I know what you are thinking "but if I am unusual, then how will I even have a market?" Here's a secret. Well, it actually isn't much of a secret at all. Millions upon millions of people are online every day. You will have a target audience. Don't fret. Someone is out there who wants to buy whatever product or service you have to offer.

Affiliate marketing sites are easy and, let's face it, we all want something easy, right? The key to making them work is to ensure they are appealing. This is what will get attention from viewers and from businesses that want to work with you.

Drop Shipping

Do you want to sell products but don't really have anywhere to keep said products? Then, drop shipping is another great option. With this type of business, you have a store front, but you don't keep the products and you don't ship them either. It works like this:

- *You set up a storefront.*
- *You take orders like any storefront would do.*
- *You collect money.*
- *You place an identical order with your distributor at a wholesale price.*
- *The distributor packs and ships the items to your customer.*
- *You get the profit (difference between your sales price and the wholesale price you paid).*

Now, here's the one downside of drop shipping. You better be 100% confident in your products because they are never in your hands. You need to know that the product you are selling is good. And you need to work with a trusted supplier who won't substitute what you think your customer is getting with something cheaper or poorly made. As the drop shipper and the owner of the storefront website, you will deal with customer service. If customers aren't happy, then it will come back on you.

The keys to a quality drop shipping business are simple:

- Offer unique products that people can't find just anywhere.
- Have a killer storefront.
- Make sure you choose quality products.
- Work with a distributor you can trust.
- Make sure you are actually making a profit.

When you do these things, you can have a successful drop shipping business.

There are some similarities between drop shipping and affiliate marketing. Neither require that you keep products on hand. However, the big difference is you will be representing yourself and your business with drop shipping. If you sell cheap products or don't offer good customer service, then this will damage your business reputation.

Otherwise, you will find drop shipping and affiliate marketing can both be easy ways to make money online. But slow down, young grasshopper. They aren't the only ways. We have many others to talk about.

Blogging – can it really work for you? Is it really all that and a bag of chips? Yes, it really can be. And, if you need proof, then consider these bloggers and how much they made in just one month, according to the Authority Hacker, a training program for blogging and earning.

Blogger	Job	Profit (March 2015)
John Lee Dumas	Podcaster, Blogger, Teacher	$232,761
Jon Dykstra	Site Builder, Blogger	$176,619
Pat Flynn	Podcaster, Blogger	$153,397
Eric James	Marketer, Coach, Blogger	$101,301
Lindsay Ostrom	Food Blogger	$32,306
Becky Mansfield	DIY Blogger	$28,200
Matt Woodward	Blogger, SEO Expert	$18,839
Michelle Gardner	Lifestyle Blogger	$17,051
Harsh Argwal	Tech Blogger	$15,313
Justin Weinger	Marketing Blogger	$9,612
Gina Horkey	Freelance Blogger	$6,595

Yes, it is possible to make money blogging. The money is there and all it requires is for you to write.

There are different ways to do this too. There are four main categories of ways to monetize a blog:

- Affiliate – You refer sales to another company through your blog and make money for those referrals.

- Advertise – You get paid to show ads on your sites. You could get paid for those ads just being there or you may get paid per click.

- Products and Services – You make money from selling on a storefront and you use your blog to drive traffic to that store.

- Content writer – You write for a company's blog as a ghostwriter and you get paid for the content. Focus for most of this section is on the other types of blogging since this doesn't drive your name recognition, but it can pay well.

Here's the cool part – all four methods work and you can use all of them at one time. The Authority Hackers looked at just the first three methods and broke down blogging profits into those three categories (they didn't analyze the fourth method, but it is included because it is a good method to employ, especially when starting out). They found that affiliate gets 31% of the profits, advertising gets 36%, and products or services gets 33%. That's a pretty even split, meaning all three methods actually do work.

How can you start making money as a blogger? Let's talk about some quick and easy tips:

- Advertise the right way. If you put ads all over the place, then people will get turned off by your blog. Use Google AdSense, eBay Affiliates, Pay-Per-Post, or Amazon Associates so that you are working with a trusted company as well.

- Link your blog to drop shipping. If you don't want to keep products on hand, you can use drop shipping and use your blog to drive traffic to your storefront. Just make sure the blog itself isn't just one massive sales pitch. That won't go over well.

- Review products. You can actually get paid for doing this. Just do as I suggested already – be honest with your reviews. Being fake will give you a bad reputation and no one will come to your website.

- Use your blog to push an eBook. Essentially, the blog itself could provide little snippets of information to draw the audience in so they will be interested in purchasing the eBook itself.

- Add a donation button. You can encourage your readers to donate money so you can keep your blog up and running. Make sure the donation button links to a trusted payment site like PayPal for best results.

The key to making money while blogging is to always ensure you are providing quality information. If you put junk out there, you will turn people off. And it will not be successful.

If you don't feel like you are a very good writer, then you may wish to consider hiring a freelance writer. These people specialize in providing quality information that will keep readers coming back for more.

You will also want to ensure that you are using SEO principles. For your blog to be successful, you have to make it findable in search engines like Google and Bing. Search engine optimization has to be a priority.

Blogging is great because it is so versatile. You can use it to boost your own business. You can get paid to boost someone else's. You can even get paid for including ads on the site. The options are endless.

Common Blogging Mistakes to Avoid

Even if you consider yourself a fantastic blogger, you could still be making mistakes for your business. That's because professional blogging is quite different than blogging about what your dog did with its new toy or a new recipe you tried for your Paleo diet. Avoid the following mistakes so that you can become a blogging aficionado.

Mistake One: Inconsistency

How do you think you look if you blog once this week, three times next week, and then not again until next month? You won't look professional! And when you leave big spaces between your blogs, people will forget about you. Consistency is your best friend when you are blogging to make money, whether you are trying to get people to go to your website or you are selling advertising space. You have to put information out there to get people to read.

Before you even start the blog, write out a schedule. Decide how often you want to post entries and then choose a time during the day to get it done. For example, you could blog three times a week on Monday, Wednesday, and Friday. No matter your schedule, just make sure you have one.

Mistake Two: Narcissism

One of the worst things you could do for your blog is talk about yourself or your business constantly. When you do, this is what readers will see:

> *"Me, me, me. Buy from me. Buy this now. I think you need it. Me. I am awesome for offering this to you. Blah, blah, blah. Me, me, me."*

That's not going to attract readers and any readers you already have will go away. You need to focus on the reader. What would they want to read? They want:

- Interesting Stories
- Answers to Questions
- Solutions to a Need
- Educational Articles
- How-Tos
- Funny Things

Focus on the reader, not yourself, if you want to get people to stick around.

Mistake Three: Boring Titles

They all tell you to not judge a book by its cover, but we are all guilty of doing just that. And your blog title is your cover. It is what will get readers intrigued. It is what will be picked up by search engines. If it is boring or weak, you won't get attention.

Mistake Four: No Images

People like pictures. Images capture attention. They intrigue people. They give them a reason to find out more. If you have ever been on a blog that had no images, then you probably immediately thought about how boring it was. If you didn't, well props to you for being in the minority. A relevant image is a must in a blog. There are different ways you can get images whether you want to pay or not:

- Flickr Creative Commons – You can use these as long as you give credit to the owner.
- Wikimedia Commons – Again, you have to give credit.
- iStockPhoto – These cost money, but they are high quality and professional.
- BigStockPhoto – This is another charge by photo site, but the cost may be worth it.

Just make sure you offer people something to look at if you want them to go on and read your blog. Note a caveat to this: Certain blog types, such as academic blogs, may not require an image, but they also may not make much money.

Fact is, pictures grab attention and make people want to read – just be sure your picture fits the content. Having a picture that makes no sense with the content can be just as damaging as having no picture at all.

Mistake Five: No Call to Action

Every good blog should have some action for the reader to take. It can be virtually anything, but a good call to action is a must to keep the reader moving forward and possibly building up ROI (Return on Investment). Need some call to action ideas?

- Contact us.
- Read my other blog.
- Check out this product.
- Learn more on our website.
- Comment below and tell us what you think.
- Think you know someone who would be interested? Share here.

Just give them some sort of action to take. Guided action works much better than just leaving them on their own.

Mistake Six: No Search Engine Optimization

How do you think search engines find you? It's not by magic. There is no fairy godmother waving around a wand at Google headquarters. There is no genie in a bottle at Bing. Search engines find you through SEO – search engine optimization. Your blogs have to be optimized to get picked up.

This means using keywords smartly throughout the content.

This means using an SEO friendly title.

It also means tagging pictures and the blog itself, categorizing it, listing keywords etc.

Now, on a side note – don't go crazy with the keywords. 1% of the text is enough. If you just fill it with keywords, then you will actually be penalized in the search engines. Yeah, they are pretty smart about it.

Mistake Seven: Ignoring Comments

Just like you absolutely must interact with people on social media, you should also respond to any comments on your blog posts. It is a great way to engage your audience and it will show that you actually care about your readers. You need to respond to good and bad comments, by the way.

Dealing with negative situations will show that you are interested in offering better. Interacting at all will build relationships between you and potential customers. When people see that you actually do respond, they will be much more likely to comment too.

Mistake Eight: Outsourcing to Poor Writers

Now, let me make one thing clear here. There are different types of outsourcing: the good, the bad, and the ugly.

- The Good – You know you aren't a good writer, so you hire a freelance ghostwriter. They are accomplished, able, and they create well thought out quality blogs for your site.
- The Bad – You hire one of the cheaper in-country freelancers because you are trying to save money. Their writing is okay, but it isn't as interesting as you had hoped and you keep finding grammatical errors.
- The Ugly – You go very cheap and hire someone in another country. They claim to be an English writer, but they don't speak the language very well and that translates into your blog posts with broken sentences, things that don't make much sense, and poorly spelled words.

If you go with the good when you know writing is not your strong point, then you have made a good decision. If you choose the bad or the ugly, you are going to shoot yourself in the foot with the blog.

Vlogs/YouTube Channels

There's a reason why videos are successful and, as they say, "the proof is in the pudding" or, well, the proof is in some words I am about to type.

- YouTube is the number two most searched website in the world. That means people go to YouTube…a lot.

- The Red Bull YouTube channel alone has more than 3.8 million subscribers.

- Videos are getting more and more popular. In fact, branded videos are getting bigger by the minute and their viewers increased 73% just from 2013 to 2014.

- Digital video Kickstarter campaigns are infinitely more popular than the campaigns that do not use video at all.

What can we learn from this?

People like videos.

Videos engage a person's visual side. They like seeing something instead of just reading words. And this is yet another way you can make money through vlogs and YouTube.

How does it work then? Let's break it down, step by step.

- You need a YouTube account. That's step one. You can do it for free and all you need to do is either create a new account altogether or link your Google account.

- Once you are in your account, look at the upper right part of the screen and click on YouTube Settings. Then choose Monetization. Then, click Enable Monetization.

- You will have a choice to click on "How Will I Be Paid". You are going to need to connect an AdSense account. Not sure how to do that? It's pretty easy and Google explains it pretty well.

- Record your video and then upload it. When you upload it, make sure you choose Submit for Revenue Sharing. Make sure you fill out all of the information requested.

That's really all there is to it. Of course, for your video to be successful, you need to market it. And that includes getting it on social media, blogging about it, linking it in forums, etc. Get it out there as much as possible.

What do you record then? That's a good question. Your vlogs or advertising videos on YouTube can be all sorts of things. Instead of focusing on subjects, I want to focus on a few characteristics of a killer video. That will help you more than anything.

1. Your video should be well-planned out. Once it is recorded, you can't change it, so you need to make it good in the first place. Objectives should include: branding, advertising, lead generation, education, sales, and endorsement.

2. Get quality production. You don't have to pay loads of money, but you do need to make sure the video looks good. If you record something that looks like crap, no one will want to watch it. It's not required to buy all the high quality equipment, especially if you want

to do a vlog. However, if you are planning an advertising video, you may wish to rent a studio or equipment.

3. Keep your video short. People don't have especially long attention spans, so don't make your video long and boring – you will lose them. Record a video that's three or four minutes long.

4. Make sure you distribute your video well. You can't just throw it up on YouTube and hope for the best. If you want to make money, people have to watch it. You need to distribute your video on your website, on your blog, on an RSS feed, and on social media sites such as Facebook, Twitter, and LinkedIn.

5. Make your video interactive. This is the key to getting attention. You need interactive links, calls to action, clickable screens, comment forms, and even live chats for discussions.

6. Make sure your video appeals to emotions. This is a big one. If you want people to take action from your video and you want to keep attention throughout the whole thing, then you need to make them happy, sad, angry, warm, etc. Appealing to emotions will absolutely help make your video successful.

Will you have a viral video like "What Does the Fox Say?" or "Gangnam Style"? Probably not. But, you can make money from videos and vlogs.

And just as with regular blogs, be sure you post videos regularly to keep attention. If you are sporadic or go away for long periods of time, then people will forget you and any online presence you had built up will go away pretty quickly. In fact, many of the mistakes listed above under blogging would apply for vlogs and YouTube.

Podcasting

Then, there are podcasts. I bet you didn't realize you could make money with them. It's actually a pretty cool option because so many people use podcasting for their passion in the first place. They started one of these for no other reason than they wanted too.

However, when you are doing something you love, you can make money from it too. Let me explain how:

- You can get sponsors. When you promote your podcasts and promote your impressions, you will start to get attention. And that can bring in sponsorships.

- You can get affiliates. You can choose products to recommend on your podcasts and affiliate companies will be glad to pay you to do just that.

- You can become a product reseller. And, when you sell products for someone else, you can make podcasts about those products – how-to, secrets, new products – all make great fodder for your videos.

- You can create courses. If there is something you can teach people, then you can invest with time, create training courses, and get 100% profit when people buy your podcasts.

- You can offer various coaching services. It may take some time before your podcasts catch on, but when they do, this can be very profitable.

Do you want to see how this is all done? Then, you need to start watching the Entrepreneur on Fire podcasts.

This is a series of daily chats that John Lee Dumas has with various entrepreneurs. It is a great way to get actionable advice that will help you make smart decisions.

> *"Each episode brings you a successful entrepreneur who shares their journey: their failures, Ah-Ha moments, successes, and much more. Each episode ends with the Lightning Round where John extracts priceless resources and action steps for you."*

Entrepreneur on Fire also offers a free podcast course called "Learn How to Create, Grow, and Monetize YOUR Podcast in 15 Days!" It would be worth your time.

You can sell ad space on your website. There are different ways you can do this, including the following:

- Google AdSense
- BuySellAds
- Puxee
- AdSella
- Advertise Space
- Project Wonderful
- Sponsored Reviews
- Blog Ads
- Ad Engage
- Digital Point
- OIO Publisher PlugIn

It is a good idea to ensure you choose a company that is reputable and that will serve your website the best.

Many More

I have honestly just tapped the surface of what the Internet offers you. I am not kidding or exaggerating. There are many more ways that the Internet and eCommerce can be good for you as a Millennial attempting to become financially free. Without going to in-depth, here are just some of the other ways you can make money on the Internet:

- Website Building. (Go back and look at that list of financially successful bloggers. The second highest paid one is a website builder too).

- B2B Marketing. (That stands for business to business).

- Google AdSense for your website. (Advertising is essential – so is doing it right).

- Become an Amazon Associate. (See affiliate niche marketing again for more tips).

- Find company referral programs. (It really is about connections afterall).

- Use Klout to track social media marketing. (It is essential to know the outcome of your actions).

- Sell on eBay. (Yes, it still exists and is still a place for making money).

- Sell on the Amazon Marketplace. (There are rules, but it is a money making giant).

- Sell on Etsy. (Especially if you are crafty and have homemade things).

- Use Amazon Mechanical Turk for crowd sourcing. (Get the word out).

- Start a Kickstarter campaign. (Have others invest in you and your ideas).

And, of course, promote yourself on social media no matter what you choose to do in order to make money online.

The thing is the Internet is huge. It is so close to being infinite it is hard for us to even understand it. So, never feel like you have limits when it comes to making money online. It's just a matter of choosing the right methods.

Low Cost of Entry

I mentioned earlier that the cost of beginning in online money making endeavors and eCommerce is low, especially compared to Real Estate and Market Investments. For the most part, it doesn't take that much money to actually get started making money online. That's the beauty of it. There are some expenses though (all tax deductible, of course). For instance, you may need to pay to register your domain and get a web host for a website. Other expenses could include social media advertising, web design costs if you need help, freelance writing expenses if you need help with that, and so on.

However, when you compare these costs to the costs of starting a brick and mortar store, getting started online is relatively low. You can easily get started for a few hundred dollars or less.

Domain Name	$15.00	Property Cost	$80,000
Hosting Account	$15.00/month	Down Payment	X 20%
WordPress Theme	$55.00	(Required)	$16,000
Random Plugin	$17.00		
Total Investment (First Month)	**$102.00**	**Total Investment (First Month)**	**$16,000**

And when it comes to the ideas I have already talked about, such as Real Estate, getting started in the online world is just cheaper. This chart shows a comparison between an online business and investing in Real Estate.

Now, don't get me wrong. I am a huge proponent of Real Estate investing. I have said that time and again. It's my favorite method and I think it has a lot of potential. It also costs a lot of money, though.

If we are realistic for a minute, you aren't going to have all that money right from the get-go, especially not after you just got done getting yourself financially free. You can't go right back into debt, and that money has to come from somewhere.

I recommend using Real Estate after you have gotten your feet wet in other ways and you have built up cash flow. Then, you can get into the heavy duty property investments. For now, though, online and eCommerce options offer some pretty sweet deals. You can make good money and not have to invest all that much. For the beginner, it is honestly what I recommend.

Remember though, like anything it does take research, due diligence, and actually doing the necessary work.

Not So Passive

Now, here's the thing. If you want truly passive income, you aren't exactly going to find it here. With some of the other methods we have discussed, you can truly sit back, earn money, and do nothing. That's not the case with the online world. You will need to maintain your website. You will need to blog or post on social media or both.

You are going to need to do at least *some* work. However, there is a really good trade off. You will be able to work from virtually anywhere as long as you have an Internet connection.

Want to go home for the holidays? You can!

Want to sip Mai Tais on a beach in Hawaii? You can!

Want to see the world? You can!

That's the great trade off with making your money online. You can work anywhere. You just need a laptop and an Internet connection of some type. Just imagine the kind of life you can live like this. It sounds pretty amazing doesn't it?

But let me get something straight right now: the more you work at an online business, the more money you can make. It offers passive income to some level, but the less passive you are, the more you can make.

What you put into it is what you will get back.

Be willing to work hard at it and enjoy the benefits. No matter what, you will enjoy a great work/life balance when you invest in the Internet through the methods we have talked about here.

Need Inspiration?

Okay, so now you know how great eCommerce can be. But...

Where do you begin?

I know that's what is going through your mind.

"Yeah, right. You are telling me to find a niche, but how do I find that niche?"

It's a reasonable question and I don't blame you for asking. The answer is research. Well, yes, research is good, but also you can check out this easy way to find inspiration:

This is a great way to get all sorts of information. You can even take a quick quiz to match you up with different online business options. Beyond that, they regularly post articles on different opportunities as well.

And you can sign up for different courses and programs as they become available. It's a great way to learn about your online options whether you are just getting started or you have a foot firmly in online business and you just want to add something new.

That way, you have something you can reference so that you don't feel overwhelmed.

We have gone over the options available and talked so much about becoming a Retired Millennial that I want to get back to the basics and remind you of what this whole thing has been about.

Chapter Thirteen:

Reiteration of Purpose

Well, we have come to nearly the end of this book. I humbly hope it has provided you with the information that you wanted to learn.

I think it is helpful to go back over the whole purpose of this, which can be summed up with one phrase – you can be a retired Millennial just like I am. Sounds great, doesn't it? Well, this isn't one of those situations where it sounds too good to be true. It can be true if you make the decision to make it happen, do the research, find what you are passionate about it, and rock it with it due diligence (and maybe a bit of work to begin), then you can be a retired Millennial.

I want to briefly reiterate everything I have already said just one more time to make sure I get my point across.

We Become Financially Free

We are young, but does that mean we have to work our fingers to the bone at a 9 to 5 job and hope we get to retire at age 70? That's just not an idea I choose to believe in. And, beyond that, I know it isn't true.

When you make financial freedom your goal, then you can achieve it. And when you reach financial freedom, you can enjoy retirement from the old grind sooner than you imagined.

But here's the thing to remember: it is all about how much you are willing to put into it. You devote the right time to your efforts and you will see results. If you devote 30 seconds every day, don't be surprised when nothing happens.

I urge you then.

Devote the time.

Believe in what you are doing.

Enjoy amazing results.

And become a financially free Millennial.

The Time It Takes Is Based on Your Willingness

How much time will it take to become financially free? Well, the answer depends on a number of factors. Of course, how much money you owe on various things will have a lot to do with it. But, the big issue is your own willingness.

Are you willing to put your all into it?

Then, you can cut down your time immensely. The more willing you are the quicker you will see results. That is absolutely the bottom line.

Of course, I would venture to guess that you wouldn't be reading this book if you weren't already pretty willing.

Learn from Others

The great thing about the path you are taking is that you have the chance to learn from others who have already accomplished financial freedom (like me). When you are getting started with this, don't get too big for your britches. In fact, that applies to everyone no matter how experienced they are. There is always a chance to learn from others.

I may be writing this book, but there is something I can learn from someone who has more knowledge and experience than me.

You have to become a sponge for information. Soak up everything you can learn, wherever you can learn it. Seek out people who have become financially free and find out how they did it. You would be surprised at how willing they will be to share information.

Become a Mentor

Once you have accomplished your own financial freedom, remember that there are many people who want to follow in your footsteps. Remember all those others that helped you in one way or another.

It's time to pay it forward.

You can become a mentor to those who are behind you and then they can learn from everything you have done and accomplished.

Don't just sit back and expect them to find you either. Put yourself out there and let people know you are willing to help them.

The good thing about this is while you are helping others with your knowledge and experience. You will still be learning too.

Invest in Yourself

When you are just starting the journey, the learning curve is steep. I haven't lied to you about that. There are things that are going to confuse you. There are things you won't understand. There will even be times when you get overwhelmed.

That doesn't mean you should stop going.

Just take the time to invest in yourself. That's because you are your future. Invest your time into learning more. Sometimes, you may even invest money in it. Just take the steps to get really involved in the areas that interest you the most. That's the key to being successful. And the more you learn, the more than learning curve will sort itself out.

The End?

Is this the end?

Of course, it isn't, not really!

It may be the end of the book, but it is hardly the end of your journey. You have a very long way to go especially if you are just getting started. It is a very exciting journey you are embarking on. It is going to be full of twists and turns, new things, discoveries about yourself and about your future, and so much more.

I just hope there are a few certain things that you have gleaned from this book and since I believe in beating a dead horse, I am going to say them one last time:

- Your journey to the New Retirement begins with financial freedom. That means pay off your debts!
- When you are ready to move forward 100% debt free, then find your passion.
- Choose something you are actually interested in so that it will never feel like work.
- Invest your time. You are worth it, aren't you? Of course you are!
- Be willing to take risks. Any type of investment is going to come with risk. That's just a part of getting the reward. Don't be afraid.
- It is all about the cash flow. If you don't have it, then you don't truly have financial freedom.
- Always research and then research some more. The more you learn, the further you will go.

With all that in mind, you are ready to go out there and become a retired Millennial. And you know right where to start – paying off your debts. It is just a matter of getting up and getting it done.

So, now shut off your computer or tablet or smartphone and start working on your budget (well, you could keep one of those devices on if that's where you will be writing your budget).

Good luck and happy retirement!

About the Author

Alex Howell is financially free and living the life of a Retired Millennial.

{NEED MORE DETAILS ABOUT YOU HERE this section could also be a brief 3 to for lines and put on the page with the copyright statement}

Sources

Authority Hacker. 2015. "Money Blogging: 23 Bloggers Analysed." *Authority Hacker*, March 2015. http://www.authorityhacker.com/make-money-blogging/

Bump, Philop. 2014. "Here Is Where Each Generation Begin and Ends, According to Facts." *The Atlantic*, 25 March 2015. http://www.theatlantic.com/national/archive/2014/03/here-is-when-each-generation-begins-and-ends-according-to-facts/359589/

Clothier, Chris. 2015. "5 Dangerous Real Estate Investing Myths Beginning Investors Believe." Bigger Pockets, 23 January 2015.
https://www.biggerpockets.com/renewsblog/2015/01/23/dangerous-real-estate-investing-myths-beginning-investors-believe/

CNN Money. 2016. "What Are Dividends." *CNN Money*.
http://money.cnn.com/retirement/guide/investing_stocks.moneymag/index3.htm

Dallett, Lydia. 2014. "Hard Charging Baby Boomers May Never Leave Their Jobs." Business Insider, January 2014: http://www.businessinsider.com/baby-boomers-work-longer-delay-retirement-2014-1

Dictionary. N.d. "Definition of retired." http://dictionary.reference.com/browse/retired

Dumas, John Lee. 2016. "Entrepreneurs On Fire Podcasts." *Stitcher,* various dates.
http://www.stitcher.com/podcast/entrepreneur-on-fire-tim-ferriss-other-incredible-entrepreneurs

Google. 2016. "Make money with AdSense." *Google*.
https://support.google.com/customsearch/answer/70347?hl=en

Harmer, Siobhan. N.d. "10 Reasons Why Following Your Passion Is More Important Than Money." Lifehack. http://www.lifehack.org/articles/money/10-reasons-why-following-your-passion-more-important-than-money.html

Lim, Melchor. 2016. "Melchor Lim quote." Quotes of All Time.
http://quotesofalltime.com/quote/remember-every-worthwhile-venture-in-life.html

Investopedia. 2016. "Be a Better Futures Trader." *Investopedia.*
http://www.investopedia.com/articles/optioninvestor/09/be-a-better-futures-trader.asp

Investopedia. 2016. "Bond Basics: What Are Bonds?" *Investopedia.*
http://www.investopedia.com/university/bonds/bonds1.asp

Investopedia. 2016. "Cash Flow." *Investopedia.*
http://www.investopedia.com/terms/c/cashflow.asp

Investopedia. 2016. "Futures." *Investopedia.* http://www.investopedia.com/terms/f/futures.asp

Investopedia. 2016. "Mutual Funds: What Are They?" *Investopedia.*
http://www.investopedia.com/university/mutualfunds/mutualfunds.asp

Investopedia. 2016. "Options Basics: What Are Options?" *Investopedia.*
http://www.investopedia.com/university/options/option.asp

Investopedia. 2016. "Stock Basics: What Are Stocks?" *Investopedia.*
http://www.investopedia.com/university/stocks/stocks1.asp

Kerpen, Dave. 2014. "How to Make Money Blogging on LinkedIn." Inc., 4 March 2014.
http://www.inc.com/dave-kerpen/how-to-make-money-by-blogging-on-linkedin.html

Lewis, Daniel J. 2015. "How podcasters are making money with podcasting." *The Audacity Podcast*, 19 January 2015. http://theaudacitytopodcast.com/how-podcasters-are-making-money-with-podcasting-tap206/

Perman, Cindy. 2013. "Are Millennials Really the 'Me' Generation?" *USA Today*, 24 August 2013. http://www.usatoday.com/story/money/business/2013/08/24/millenials-time-magazine-generation-y/2678441/

Ramsey, Dave. N.d. "How the Debt Snowball Method Works." *Dave Ramsey.*
http://www.daveramsey.com/blog/how-the-debt-snowball-method-works

Schroer, William J. N.d. "Generations X,Y, Z and the Others." The Social Librarian.
http://www.socialmarketing.org/newsletter/features/generation1.htm

Sightings, Tom. 2012. "Will Social Security Be There for You?" U.S. News and World Report, 10 July 2012. http://money.usnews.com/money/blogs/on-retirement/2012/07/10/will-social-security-be-there-for-you

Sweeney, Ash. N.d. "Ash Sweeney quote." Unknown source location.

Tabaka, Marla. 2015. "9 Networking Tops to Make Money of Facebook." *Inc.*, 19 January 2015. http://www.inc.com/marla-tabaka/9-networking-tips-to-make-money-on-facebook.html

United States Department of Labor. 2016. "Labor Force Statistics from the Current Population Survey." Bureau of Labor Statistics, United States Department of Labor. http://data.bls.gov/timeseries/LNS14000000

Yerian, Nathan. 2014. "10 Common Mistakes Most Business Bloggers Make." *Hubspot*, 14 January 2014. http://blog.hubspot.com/insiders/blogging-mistakes

www.ingramcontent.com/pod-product-compliance
Lightning Source LLC
Chambersburg PA
CBHW021942170526
45157CB00003B/891